ANNA ATKINSON

The Wonky Woman's Guide To Tarot

Copyright © 2020 by Anna Atkinson

All rights reserved. No part of this publication may be reproduced, stored or transmitted in any form or by any means, electronic, mechanical, photocopying, recording, scanning, or otherwise without written permission from the publisher. It is illegal to copy this book, post it to a website, or distribute it by any other means without permission.

First edition

ISBN: 979-8-56-258666-7

Editing by Triston Spicer

This book was professionally typeset on Reedsy. Find out more at reedsy.com

Contents

Introduction		vi
1	The Fool	1
2	The Magician	5
3	The High Priestess	10
4	The Empress	14
5	The Emperor	18
6	The Hierophant	23
7	The Lovers	27
8	The Chariot	32
9	Strength	37
10	The Hermit	41
11	The Wheel	44
12	Justice	48
13	The Hanged Man	52
14	Death	56
15	Temperance	61
16	The Devil	65
17	The Tower	70
18	The Star	74
19	The Moon	77
20	The Sun	81
21	Judgement	86
22	The World	90
23	Ace of Wands	94
24	2 of Wands	99
25	3 of Wands	102

26	4 of Wands	106
27	5 of Wands	109
28	6 of Wands	114
29	7 of Wands	119
30	8 of Wands	122
31	9 of Wands	126
32	10 of Wands	131
33	Knave of Wands	134
34	Knight of Wands	137
35	Queen of Wands	140
36	King of Wands	144
37	Ace of Cups	148
38	2 of Cups	151
39	3 of Cups	155
40	4 of Cups	160
41	5 of Cups	164
42	6 of Cups	169
43	7 of Cups	172
44	8 of Cups	176
45	9 of Cups	180
46	10 of Cups	184
47	Knave of Cups	188
48	Knight of Cups	192
49	Queen of Cups	197
50	King of Cups	201
51	Ace of Swords	205
52	2 of Swords	209
53	3 of Swords	213
54	4 of Swords	217
55	5 of Swords	221
56	6 of Swords	225
57	7 of Swords	229
58	8 of Swords	233

59	9 of Swords	237
60	10 of Swords	242
61	Knave of Swords	246
62	Knight of Swords	249
63	Queen of Swords	252
64	King of Swords	256
65	Ace of Pentacles	260
66	2 of Pentacles	263
67	3 of Pentacles	266
68	4 of Pentacles	270
69	5 of Pentacles	276
70	6 of Pentacles	280
71	7 of Pentacles	284
72	8 of Pentacles	288
73	9 of Pentacles	292
74	10 of Pentacles	297
75	Knight of Pentacles	301
76	Knave of Pentacles	304
77	Queen of Pentacles	307
78	King of Pentacles	311
	Afterword	315
	Acknowledgements	317
	Teacher Acknowledgment	320

Introduction

As a trained Trans-personal Arts Counsellor, I have always had an interest in archetypes. For years I have run art and story workshops on ancient myths and fairy tales. I've dabbled with the Tarot on and off for a number of years. This year in January, on the way to somewhere, I found a completely new, old deck in a charity shop. I had a four hour train journey ahead of me, so I sat and I shuffled and played with the cards.

It's as if some magical fairy dust was sprinkled on me because from that point on, I was hooked. The whole year became a tribute to Tarot. I painted my own deck, wrote my first ever book (which is in your glorious hands), did a zillion readings for people, and wrote my first one-woman show about - you've guessed it - Tarot. I did this on top of teaching full-time, dealing with the effects of a global pandemic and seeing clients in the evenings.

I'd love to take the credit for all this, but really it was the Tarot that took me on a journey and this wild adventure. I picked a card each day and wrote, painted, played and pondered. Bizarrely enough, the Tarot actually took me into a very timeless space even though my schedule was jam-packed.

The thing about the Tarot is that it is a living, breathing entity. Like all archetypal things it becomes alive in you. The cards meet you in the most mysterious ways and they speak directly to you. They help you slow down, take stock and they can be great grounding anchors or gentle soul nudges. Sometimes they beckon you towards your future or maybe take you back to the past to what you need to remember. They allow you to meet with your wild twin within. The one who breaks all the rules and eats chocolate cake for breakfast.

As much as its's wonderful to do readings and look up the meanings, its also vital that you let the cards live through your daily experiences and speak to you.

I highly recommend creating your own deck as a way of letting the Tarot come alive in you. Underneath my wonky woman's Tarot journal entry I have included journal prompts for you to consider.

I am deeply grateful to you for purchasing this book. It has been a very big dream of mine to write and illustrate for a very long time and until now I never made space for it in my busy life.

The Tarot helped me create that space.

You can read this book in a linear way or if you have your own deck you can pull a card each day and look it up, or just flip open the book at a random page and see where you land.

At some point I may publish this as a card deck so watch this space. Feel free to identify yourself as a fellow wonky woman and message me any art, writing or fabulous insights or feedback at https://m.me/wonkywomenoftarot.

You can also like my Facebook page **Wonky Woman Cauldron** to hear more about my work with healing art and everyday enchantment or leave a dazzling or dastardly Amazon review.

This process of journaling your own deck will move mountains in your life and connect you directly to your hearts deepest dreams and desires.

It will create poetry and miracles in your life as well as help you recognize all the ways in which these archetypes live through your precious beating heart.

May this book bring light to the dark and difficult days. There is always treasure in that dark.

Anna xxx

Oct 2020

* * *

Knocking on the door of creative abundance
It never quite lets me in
Its like my key is rusty
Gets jammed in the lock
It's time to change things
Move through this really painful threshold
Oil those creaks
Those feelings that I am not enough
I am
I am golden light
And I allow love in
I allow richness to flow
For the thick door to slide open
And for me to walk through it
Knowing all of my worth

* * *

Self Portrait

1

The Fool

Innocence Folly

The fool who persists in his folly will become wise.

-William Blake

The Fool is my favourite card and also, some say, the most powerful card in the deck.

This card really takes me back to my wonderful therapy training journey.

On the first day of my 3-year therapy training, we made fool's hats out of newspapers and feathers. This was in order to get silly and foolish from the off so that we set the tone for mistakes, awkwardness and humour further down the line.

In these grave times, humour is perhaps our only salvation.

There have been times with clients when I have been utterly at a loss of what to do or say because of the devastation of a young person's situation. Then someone in the group farts and just for a moment the trauma cloud bursts (and a new type of cloud enters), we all laugh until our sides hurt and someone else laughs so hard they fart too.

I guess I wanted to write this book with some trace of foolishness. Many books I read, that often have quite good advice, say it in such a serious way that I can't even take it in.

Humans need the humour hummus which is the opposite of the Kool Aid. Maybe that's why cat videos always trump inspirational quotes.

   If only cats could be 'couch coaches' and purrr out inspirational quotes in lilac Helvetica.

- Nine Steps to shinier whiskers
- 'Follow your Dreamies' (Dreamies is a cat biscuit brand – it's basically cat heroin – that cats would gladly trade *all* 9 lives and an ear for)
- How to be aloof on a first date (and every other date)

The fool actually doesn't have a cat, but a small excitable dog. He moves through a threshold and is blind. He gives no fucks about his lack of outer vision.

He's likely to have some sort of map drawn by children with purple crayon on the inside of his eyelids. I imagine he's whistling.

By the end of his journey he'll attract all sorts of other passing creatures: newts, ocelots and neon parakeets, like a living Quentin Blake drawing.

As I write, I have a stinking cold and I don't want to go on any journeys, especially not ones where I can't open my eyes, it's bad enough not being able to breath through my nose.

At some point though we all have to say 'sod it' and risk looking like a fool for love. If we don't we'll end up being in relationship with nothing but our cat.

Or worse, having only a pastel mug, with an inspirational quote on, to clutch during the storms.

* * *

- **How can you be more silly?**
- **Wear something ridiculous**
- **Go to a laughter yoga class**
- **Eat something you loved as a child**
- **Paint with your non dominant hand**

2

The Magician

Mastery/Trickery

I was a magician's assistant and had to go in the box that they put the swords through, and there's no trick to it. You literally have to dodge the swords.

-Caroline Flack

This is the archetype I made room for when I went 50% self employed last year.

Not 100% though, because I don't want to be homeless again. My Mum can't have me back in her teeny damp spare room with peeling 80's Laura Ashley wallpaper, aged nearly 40. Also my husband would miss me making a giant mess around him.

I had dreamt it would be this wonderful world of drinking flat whites with a tiny silver chrome laptoppy notebook in cafés where oat milk comes as standard and the brownies contain some sort of Mayan cocaine (for working laptop people who are dressed like they have a stylist who picks out their clothes).

Nope. It's me in my coffee stained pyjamas with my ancient student Toshiba laptop that turns itself off periodically and is only one model away from still having a floppy disc slot.

I'm swearing at it. It's 10.30 at night. I want to go to bed and I'm sending emails about what types of crayons we are using on Wednesday; and whether or not my arts for wellbeing session will interrupt the special assembly about internet safety.

Maybe if I'd learnt about internet safety I wouldn't have tried to sell my soul on 'find a therapist.com' in a dodgy font next to a stock photo of a tree with an empty bench next to it, on a matt finish flyer because no-one wants a shiny therapist.

I have to work even when I get sick and I get sick because I work about 9 days per week. The wolves are at my door and the wand ain't working (or mouse for that matter).

'Turn it off and on again you Windows 95 bastard!'

Nah its great. I'm my own boss. Which just means I swear at myself more and don't have a water filter to procrastinate by.

I have hope for the purple cape. I mean I can totally wear one now, on the days I am self employed, no-one will tell me off.

I am learning now to spin many plates, let lots crash on the floor and only pick out the broken china I really need to save and piece together.

That's not what motivational coaches say is it?

No they normally have faces that suggest they actually live in the internet.

THE MAGICIAN

The trick my cool taxi driver man said to me today (because I'm such a failure that I still can't drive): 'the trick is to be prepared to take yourself seriously' he said.

I know I've got magic and I take that seriously, I thought.

That's why I write about tarot and have an altar in every room.

Why I chose the first aid kit of writing daily poetry and making art instead of getting an office job (Although my inner magician would love a swivel chair).

Why I refuse to wear anything but red shoes everyday and always have hair that looks like a wild bird's nest. I use stationary supplies to make offerings to the Gods of Magic.

And my cooking is often as awful as a dodgy spell. Vegan toad in the hole. With more hole than toad and a couple of vegans thrown in for good measure.

I always need to remember that at the end of the day I am *not* my own boss. The *magic* is my boss.

The wonderful, diverse clients that come to me. The strange contracts I sometimes get (currently running a weird geo-cache project - even though I can't ever find my own keys). The kooky adverts I reply to and books and courses that the universe shuffles me onto.

Life tricks us and mastery is an illusion but I'd rather use real blackberries in a spell than a Blackberry device any day.

Purple juice smeared on my purple cape; no-one can tell, it all just blends in. No need for Vanish. Magic!

* * *

- How can you bring enchantment into everyday life?
- Who would you turn into a toad?
- Who would you be a fairy godmother to?
- What would be your 3 wishes whispered to a magic lamp?
- Design a spell for maximum fabulousness

3

The High Priestess

Intuition/Assumption

You have to leave the city of your comfort and go into the wilderness of your intuition. What you'll discover will be wonderful. What you'll discover is yourself.

–Alan Alda

Two poems for The High Priestess:

Red carpet

Darling I'd waltz with you all night
  Under those stars
  Doesn't matter where we are
  Part of my heart feels blighted
  Destined to hurt others
  But I want to be in my truth
  My power
  And my body
  This glorious glorious body

Help me love it again
Help me know that love and sexuality are my birth right
They are not bad
They are my prayer

* * *

In my vulnerability my safety lies

Yesterday just when i thought my week was peak crazy
It got crazier
Went to a goddess workshop (to try and be more like the lass on this card)
Got there after 7am start and we were locked out in rain
Many shuffled chairs and apologies later we went in late
Did the first bit
Experienced an altercation
Women 'triggered' by eachother
Hissing and spitting
Scouring and
Scrawling
Claws teeth and wombs

Then....

An announcement to all attendees : THE WORKSHOP HAS BEEN DOUBLE BOOKED FOR A FUNERAL. PLEASE LEAVE

Black ties
Sparkly goddesses in uncomfortably shiny lyrca
Mourning suits

Crystal decks
Coffins
Affirmations
And vegan cake amidst real tears
Not just workshop ones
An actual person died
We are not yet reborn
This word is crazy
We try and act like phoenixes
Rising
When we don't even know what its like to be real ash
Real dust
Real sorrow

* * *

- What can you do to listen to your Intuition?
- What would she say?
- What would she tell you to do?
- Write a poem from your feelings without thinking.
- Be in her tuition.

THE HIGH PRIESTESS

4

The Empress

Fertility/Overprotection

My mother told me to be a lady. And for her, that meant be your own person, be independent.

-Ruth Bader Ginsburg

I knew it was the mother card before I picked it. I felt her swollen belly stirring

I stopped writing for a day. I felt the fallow space. Letting go. Empty

I've been picking out smooth round rocks for children to paint on

Stone bellies from the seabed

Aware of huge resistance
   The acknowledgment of the lack of maternity in my unimpregnated body

I taught year 3 yesterday and felt like the bad mother. Nagging, punishing scolding, withholding

THE EMPRESS

The Empress is the good mother. She's the one who packs those lunchboxes where everything has little compartments for different healthy snacks. Squares of trimmed cucumber with the skin peeled. Sweet cherry tomatoes and triangular sandwiches of hope. She leaves kind notes under organic granola bars

She puts name tags in everything and never loses her shit

Always pregnant with an irritatingly annoying glow

I am not her. My eyes feel sunken, hair greying, skin pale and lips sore

I am more ice queen as this cold January draws out like a sword.

I am taking comfort in layers where I can hide my un holy belly and just be in some sort of dark solitude

More hermit than empress. I shy away from her golden throne preferring caves and hollows

Long jumpers and a crown made of knots

I cannot connect with this empress and her star filled head dress

As a non mother I know this would be an ideal time to perhaps acknowledge or write about my own mother but I love her so much it hurts to speak

I cannot

The umbilical cord wraps around my words and throat

I wonder about the bees
   I am not seeing enough of them

Less pollinators

I am not seeing her enough

It stings. But not like a bee sting

Its more like the sting of the being that never became

The sting of the unsung, undone, and unbecome

Blessed art thou among women,
  and blessed is the fruit
  of thy womb.

Thy womb

Pray for us sinners now,
  and at the hour of our death

Amen

* * *

- **What is your relationship with your mother like?**
- **Are you a mother?**
- **Can you tend to your un-mothered parts?**
- **Write a letter from your protective inner parent to your wounded child.**
- **Birth a new creative project that uses sensory as opposed to intellectual skills- i.e knitting, gardening, writing, baking, pampering or painting**

THE EMPRESS

5

The Emperor

Authority/Rigidity

My father, Eric Trethewey, is a poet, so I had one right inside the house. And on long trips, he'd tell me, if I got bored in the car, to write a poem about it. And I did find that poetry was a way for me, I think as it for a lot of people, to articulate those things that seem hardest to say.

-Natasha Trethewey

Its no wonder this was one of the last entries I filled in (the order these are published is not the order I wrote them).

The Emperor is the father card.

Such a painful painful wounded place. The tributary of my male lineage is very blocked.

I found out aged 10 the man who I thought was my father wasn't. This was very confusing. It wasn't until I was 22 that I decided to track down my biological dad.

It's a bit like I was one of those teddy bears with only one ear. A part of me was missing and felt debilitated.

He replied to a letter just after my 22nd birthday and we met in a very funny café in Central London called the Stock Pot, where you could get a two-course meal for £8.40 and which was "more than a café, but not quite a restaurant".

Stodgy puddings, synthetic custard, bargain roast dinners and greasy plates piled high with liver and fried onions. Roast dinners for less than £5, lasagne, fish cakes, boiled potatoes, apple crumbles drowning in Bird's custard, fruit cocktail, golden-syrup puddings.

This is quoted from a wonderful Guardian article by Rebecca Hardy, in a tribute to The Stockpot, when it finally closed its doors in 2015.

Making way for gentrification and chain restaurants with overly smiley staff.

She says that it 'belonged to an earlier world, a time before we got obsessed with celebrity chefs. It wasn't just food that was important, it was also about the experience. It was a mixed clientele, a hardcore of students, lots of people down on their luck, filling up on their one meal of the day. The atmosphere was reassuringly bohemian. Shabby and make-do, with tables pushed so close you could eavesdrop on the conversations.'

This for me was a great metaphor for the relationship between us which was about to unfold. It was exactly this. Sometimes a cheap substitute for a normal father and daughter constellation, perhaps, but always rich, warm eclectic and more about the warmth of the here-and-now company than the menu of my childhood hurts.

You seem my father is not necessarily great father material. He gets impatient very easily and doesn't much like children, however he is a *great* friend. He has and has had a great many friends. He has wonderful tales of these friendships, chance encounters and mad escapades. He's a mate you can rely on.

My father is both a poet and a storyteller, neither of things make for a reliable Dad.

But like the Stockpot there is something very human about our flawed familial situation. We sometimes don't get on. Hurts from both sides come up but then we'll go down the pub with his great gang of friends and I will forgive him and he will forgive me.

We will share a meal of microwaved macaroni and a pint of Yorkshire bitter.

Our stockpot days. My father and me, more than a café but not quite a restaurant.

***

- What is your relationship with your father like?
- How are you rigid?
- Do you have authority over your own life?
- What part of you needs fathering?
- What boundaries do you need to put in place to protect yourself?

6

The Hierophant

Faith/Fanaticism

The sense of smell, like a faithful counsellor, foretells its character.

-Jean Anthelme Brillat-Savarin

The Hierophant is related to the angel of temperance. A spiritual leader and man of great counsel. I think of Friar Lawrence from Romeo and Juliet, and we all know how that turned out.

This is my birth card. Perhaps my drive for studying counselling and therapy. My mission is to be a wise counsellor.

I had a fittingly Catholic upbringing and in my older years decided confession was a poor version of therapy.

Forgiveness, for me, is more of a conversation than a confession. Confessing suggests shame. Conversation suggests a widening of horizons and a space for mutual sharing and trust.

My Catholic roots haven't completely gone.

Two years ago I entered into a group study of the metaphysical text 'A course in Miracles.' This is the path of the Christian mystic.

It's open to all faiths. It does use scary words like God, Christ and salvation, but not in the normal sense.

In the sense that we are all of these things and capital letters are not called for.

Today's daily lesson suggested, in fact, that even inanimate objects contain traces of God. This is probably why I have so many trinkets.

Yesterday I asked my group to pick objects to represent themselves.

One person picked a tiny, round, blue box and recalled her 5 year old daughter's beautiful blue dream from the night before.

Another chose a deep purple, silk, hand-dyed scarf which she wrapped around her 'pain in the neck'.

Another picked some battery-powered electric lights which she held up as the light outside grew dim.

Objects have power.

So do men of the clergy.

Many victims and survivors have been morally and sexually objectified in the shadows of religion and church life.

Churches once open are now locked in case junkies nick the gold crucifixes to pay for fixes.

My mum still cleans her local church on a rota. She cuts fresh flowers from her garden to place in the porch at the entrance to the threshold.

THE HIEROPHANT

At the feet of God.

She blesses herself in holy water but doesn't take the sacrament because she feels like a sinner in the eyes of god.

My mother is my church. Always good. Always kind. Forever generous and warm.

Eternally loving.

I don't want any God that doesn't worship her.

*** * * ***

- **Who has given you great counsel in your life?**
- **Listen**
- **What advice do you wish you had ignored/ followed?**
- **Make an offering to the wise person inside you**
- **Ask questions**

THE WONKY WOMAN'S GUIDE TO TAROT

The Hierophant V

7

The Lovers

Unity/Obsession

Ninety-nine percent of the world's lovers are not with their first choice. That's what makes the jukebox play.

-Willie Nelson

I am sitting here on a high speed train on a beautiful but chilly sunset evening in mid-October. The sky looks ever so slightly brooding.

Like a lover who you suspect is going to break your heart... or at least sand the edges down.

This autumn might break my heart.
   I am off to visit my 90 year old dad - third attempt now and York already has an outbreak.

The chill is coming. What with this pandemic, my spells of dried-up writing and my fourth year into marriage (where we've barely left our cluttered home for months on end, except to buy cupboard goods and emergency Tunnock's teacakes). This card feels slightly irrelevant.

Get your coat love, you've pulled (the lovers card).

I used to wear my best lace knickers on dates, curl my hair and zip into tiny shimmering slip dresses effortlessly.

The other day someone from work was protesting about not having a partner.

They won't complete you I thought. You need to complete you.

Be a romancer to yo self.

Date nights. Bubble baths. Champagne. Roses. Posh chocolates. The works. All for yourself.

I haven't been doing that. I buy Aldi soup and Iceland frozen peas on a Saturday night for fuck's sake.

Usually romancing myself involves woolly socks and a tear-jerking film. Other times it involves dancing and drinking into the small hours (i.e. past 9pm) to shamanic drumming in my living room with a Bloody Mary.

It often involves me taking time out from others.

And having time in.

I've had a *lot* of time in. I'm dating my hot water bottle.
   I've put on so much weight over Covid, none of my trousers do up.

I feel frumpy and embarrassed. Long gone are my lovers days of wild passion and pizzazz.

But I did buy myself a pair of red sexy stocking tights (for plus size thighs) . Just for me.

THE LOVERS

An impulse internet purchase obvs.

I get the tummy control pants Facebook ad pop ups now.

I made a sexy video spoof during lockdown when I should have been planning an anti- bullying quiz for year six girls.

The Amazon delivery man rang my bell with a knee support band, I also ordered. And I quickly shoved on a modesty smock.

I deleted the video and ate most of a bag of tortilla chips.

I look at the Instagram girls and I feel like a far off island.

I have not been a great date to me or my husband this year.

At new year, we went to Cambridge for a 1920's speakeasy. I wore black sequins and feathers and drank pickled gin cocktails with bright painted red lips.

We danced and drank and cavorted.

And the next day, hungover, I got excited in a middle aged way about the 50% off tableware at John Lewis and the pretty front door wreaths hanging on Cambridge town houses, imagining we no longer had to rent and could buy a house with a nice front door.

Little did we know it'd be our last night out for some while.

So the lovers card this year has been a slow burner, a dull waltz and a chip butty, holding hands kind of date on a socially distanced political ice rink.

I tell my husband that if he starts getting a continuous cough he's on the sofa.

He kisses my roll of belly fat. And gives me a fuck you kiss on the forehead. We both wear woolly socks and plan not to put the heating on just yet. Hot to trot.

Oh and our front door got a lick of paint during lockdown.

* * *

- **How can you give your love life a lick of paint?**
- **Write a love letter to yourself**
- **Write a list of all past lovers**
- **How can you love yourself more today?**

THE LOVERS

VI

The LOVERS

8

The Chariot

Advancement/Heedlessness

The demons are innumerable, appear at the most inconvenient times, and create panic and terror. But I have learnt that if I can master the negative forces and harness them to my chariot, then they can work to my advantage.

–Ingmar Bergman

My chariot is less of a Lamborghini and more like a child's length of string with an economy baked beans tin can gaffa taped on the end.
   .....
   Trundle trundle.
   Today I walked home from work/ school.

Tired, with awful Lycra silver leggings because of my thigh chaffing issues, I hobble home over twigs, mud, fallen red leaves, majestic tree archways.

It takes my mind off the day and I can fade into the bracken.
   Parts of the walk contain roads and cars but the best bits are wooded.

THE CHARIOT

I love the train tracks.
   The way the rats dart before a train comes.
   The scuzzy bridges marked with graffiti.

The shrivelled blackberries that came early this year and are now mere husks.
   My chariot is not fast but slightly uneven. Black sensible trainers, customised with neon orange laces which passing teens today sniggered at.

Fuck the system guys.

Owning it with own shoelaces in non-brand trainers is the first step to rebellion surely?

I forget that youths no longer hang out in Camden market. Buying Sterling silver belly rings and herbal highs from men with terrible dreads in more terrible tie dye .
   Even fake Louis Vuitton bags from Oxford Street are long gone.

The identity of today's street kids resides only in gaming chat rooms.
   Talking to 30 year old failed you tubers called Ian.

I preferred smoking in bike sheds.
   At least you didn't need a username and password.
   Only a lighter and a pack of camel lights.

My chariot may be stalled but its got orange laces.
   I'm headed to that disco in the year 2000.

Won't it be strange when we're all fully grown.

* * *

Love is telling me....

There are two sides
And you are caught between them
Rock and hard place
But I seek something softer
More agile
Less demanding
More precious
Like the chariot pulled in opposing directions
The third way might be possible
The slither that love sometimes paves

* * *

- What trusty Steeds do you pull along from your past?
- What pulls you into your Future?
- Where are you going?
- Where have you been
- Enjoy the ride!

THE CHARIOT

VII

The Chariot

9

Strength

Assertion/Aggression

Only in art will the lion lie down with the lamb, and the rose grow without thorn.

-Martin Amis

Immediate anxiety upon pulling this card. I never face the lions.
   I get thrown to them yes. But never pet them willingly.

I am outwardly gentle and easy going.
   A lamb if you like.
   And I regularly get put in with the lions.

Lions on a power trip. They roar.
   They soar.
   They *have* to be heard and ego-stroked.

Dripping with it all at the mouth.

Big shiny manes, like they just came from the hairdresser. Marie Kondo houses with vibrators that 'spark joy'.

I'm so sick of them.

Around them I shrink and shrivel. From a gentle lamb to a tiny mouse. Their compliments are false.

Their nails fake.

I trust the woman on this card. She looks kind and gentle. Like she might remove a spike from a big paw without causing a yelp or claws to prick out.

I have to trust my gentleness in the lions den.

I am meek and mild but I am also resilient and wild. With my woolly coat and trembling blackened knees I will survive this winter and hopefully others.

I will rest and digest, flock and fleece.

Maybe I will even be shorn of my only protection.

I want to find the lion heart within my lamb body and feed it. No longer hide behind my long curly hair and woollen coats.

I don't want to be anyone's meat or sustenance. Only my own.

The lamb can't meet the lion with aggression. Only gentleness. A tiny squeak or bleat.

Like beauty and the beast maybe I need to see the best in those fanged jaws. Pulling out thorns and seeing them with eyes of love.

Others will shout 'be careful' but I know that my courage will be all I need. I approach the lion rather than it approaching me.

In every lion is a lamb. I will try to see that.

STRENGTH

* * *

- How can you speak up?
- Who is abusing their power around you?
- Who seems like a lion but is actually a lamb?
- Practice your Roar

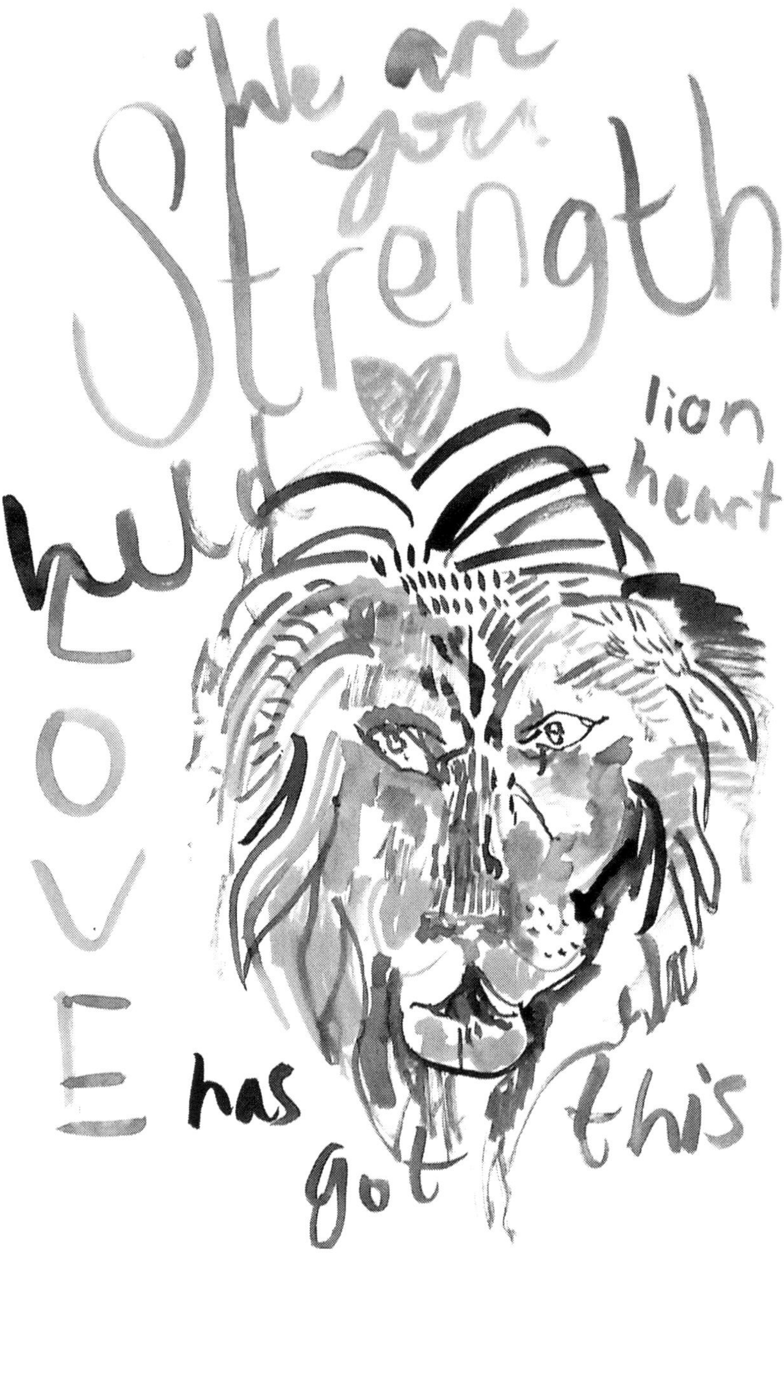
We are
Strength
lion heart
kind
LOVE
has got this

10

The Hermit

Introspection/Isolation

When the devil grows old he turns hermit.

-Ludovico Ariosto

This card is one I know pretty well. I actually have a huge devotion to this archetype. You see the thing is, I deeply trust hermits. They live from the inside.
    They are happiest in their quiet caves. They don't need entertainment. They are the kind of people you can sit in silence with and simply know they are listening.

The lantern that the Hermit carries is deeply beautiful to me. It is the whole world.

In my mind these hermits have spent so long being with their darkness and contemplating the quiet shadows of each corner that they are implicitly trustworthy.

Their pace is slow, their hair long.

Wisdom. But not ego wisdom. Something more wizened and more sober. If Jesus had grown old he would probably have looked like the Hermit. Father Christmas after he finally cut out mince pies from his diet and started embracing a more demure grey wardrobe.

The Hermit teaches me to to be alone with my self and not be lonely. My husband reminded me this week to remember to light a candle for myself.
   I spend so often lighting them for others I barely remember to do this.

So yesterday I lit a candle just simply for me. I watched it burn and felt a quietness come over me. All the to do lists in my head went out the window and for a moment I simply sat and let things be.

The wind was howling outside yet I was there with my little light.
   In truth I want the Hermit to accompany me everywhere because I feel lonely without him. Maybe I should remember that he needs me as much as I need him.
   Because as self sufficient as he is, he cannot survive in isolation.

He needs to bring his light back for others to see.

He needs to know how loved he is.

* * *

- **Enjoy a great night in**
- **Make a duvet cave**
- **Don't forget snacks**
- **Return to the village only when you are ready**

THE HERMIT

IX

The Hermit

11

The Wheel

Revolution/Repetition

Let's go 'round again
  Maybe we'll turn back the hands of time Let's go 'round again
  One more time (One more time)

- Average White Band

Sitting here amidst the news horrors I sort of wonder about turning back the hands of time. Maybe we could reverse the effects of climate change. Act sooner and stop violent computer games and sweat shops ever being invented.

As someone who works in a primary school, I often wonder whether the curriculum was better in the late 70's. At least you could do art more than once a fortnight. SATs tests hadn't come in yet.

I remember having great primary school teachers. One taught only sculpture as that was what he was interested in (luckily I liked sculpture). He'd show us slides from his trips to Italy and we would make wonderful abstract, phallic towers out of clay, cocktail sticks and drinking straws (not bottle tops as they were made of foil not plastic back then).

In order to reverse climate change we'd have to banish EasyJet and continue holidaying in Skegness. We'd need to not privatise the rail network and have kept trains romantic. Maybe then people wouldn't be so co-dependent with their Fiestas (I quite proudly at the age of 38 have never owned a car).

Though Southeastern Rail network killed my love affair with trains long ago, too many late nights on rail replacement buses that smell of dog poo.

If I could go back in time and prevent anything I think it would be the globalisation of everything.

My grandparents were my deepest inspiration, spiritually, mentally and physically. My grandad was an odd job man worked with his hands, my grandparents grew all their own food on their allotment and my nan always made anyone who popped round a bottomless brew with generous biscuits.

Their basic tiny house was always full and warm. They knew everyone on their street's middle names and they would do anything for anyone.

As long as they were together they never flew on a plane, although loved the odd coach trip. They were married for over 50 years and my grandad died at home in my nan's safe arms.

After he died she decided to visit relatives in America. A once in a life time trip. She went on a plane for the first time and ate her first pizza. When she returned she simply put the kettle on and said she was glad to be home where she could walk everywhere and taste the food she'd grown.

She never ate pizza again.

* * *

- ·What are your family patterns?
- ·Where were you this time last year?
- ·What cycles do you recognize within yourself?
- ·Observe a natural cycle in nature for a year
- ·What rhythm's/ routines support you?

THE WHEEL

The WHEEL X

47

12

Justice

Balance/Prejudice

We need to keep making our streets safer and our criminal justice system fairer – our homeland more secure, our world more peaceful and sustainable for the next generation.

-Barack Obama

Having touched on intolerance in a previous entry I am wondering when intolerance turns to prejudice.

My guess is that this happens when fear turns to trauma.

The original image on this card is quite striking. The queen in the red dress holds scales and a sword. At her feet is a blindfolded baby. She has a quite serene, Mona Lisa type expression on her face.

The serenity is at odds with her red dress and sword. The vulnerable baby is at odds with her powerful throne and crown and the scales contain a bar of gold on one side and a fish on the other.

Both weighing the same.

I guess the fishy moments in our lives are as defining as the golden ones.
   And you can't survive on gold alone, but fish finger sandwiches keep even Captain Birdseye going.

Feeling quite rotten at the moment. My cold has spread to my throat, head and limbs, everything aches and hurts ahead of 2 days of teaching. I need rest.

Writing feels really hard. Everything feels hard.
   I can't even sleep.

Maybe I'll wear red today in an effort to feel a bit better.

I guess these rotten fish scrawls will hopefully make way for some gold ones.

I feel most connected to the blindfolded baby right now. Vulnerable and in need of protection.

This year I am looking at how to wield my sword in the world. I know I need to be prepared to use it. But only if life gets really unbalanced.

Cutting ties is so painful to me but I recognize it needs to happen. I need to protect that vulnerable baby at all costs.

I feel like the woman in the dress is prepared to kill. The red dress will hide the blood stains. I hide my blood stains. My trauma. I also hide my gold and my fish.

The baby is her innocence. The only reason she'd actually kill is to be the fierce protective mother.

Throwing a fish at the attacker won't do. What if the attack is from an aggressive seal! Or a giant penguin? They'd love the fish, no?

No use throwing money at problems either. You just get broke. Then you have 99 problems and the fish ain't one. Sometimes a sword is the only way to cut through the heart of things.

It's certainly the only way we can heal trauma. We must accept a part of us has been killed off or slain and heal it by tending to our tender baby's blindness.

Our hands may be red but our blindfold is white.

Hurt people hurt people.

* * *

- **What do you need to cut to the heart of?**
- **What has happened to you that was unjust?**
- **Who do you wish revenge on?**
- **Light a forgiveness candle even if you are not quite ready to say sorry- For you and the other person**
- **Forgive yourself for something you did which was unfair to another**

JUSTICE

13

The Hanged Man

Transcendence/Treachery

When a man knows he is to be hanged in a fortnight, it concentrates his mind wonderfully.

-Samuel Johnson

Between worlds he hangs. Upside down.
   So often we are in this place.

Suspended.

In many ways this year has been a hanged man.

Arse over tit.

We are between jobs. Between our own lives. Between eachother. Between a rock and a hard place. Between clenched teeth. Between who we are and what we want to be.

Between the sheets. Between lovers. Between phone calls. Between hot and cold, night and day, winter and summer, yes and no, good and bad.

Medium rare or well done?
   Grilled or Baked?
   Eat in or Take Away?
   Single or taken?
   Meat free or Coeliac?

Life is a spectrum we are caught in the middle of and hung up by a golden thread.
   Like an artisan lightbulb on a flex above a plate of thrice-cooked chips eaten between lunch and dinner.

The betwixt and between.

Ensnared and left to dangle.

Like the fairy on top of the Christmas trees drunken upside down cousin, the Hanged Man reverses our verses.

We speak words backwards, summon riddles, and ask more questions than we seek answers.

Mirror writing on the wall.
   .llaw eht no gnitirw rorriM

The Hanged Man is not earthed, he lives between worlds.

Part of the flat earth society, a conspiracy theorist. David Blaine submerged in a box.

An offering head first from the heavens.

His name not quite marked in the register.

* * *

- **What have you started but not finished?**
- **Who are you hanging around with?**
- **Are you between two different phases?**
- **What transitions are you going through?**
- **What are you in the middle of reading?**

The Hanged Man

14

Death

Conclusion/ Reduction

Life is hard. Then you die. Then they throw dirt in your face. Then the worms eat you. Be grateful it happens in that order.

–David Gerrold

Picking the death card the morning after the sun card feels inevitable.

Feels a bit like I had such a sweet day yesterday on my birthday that I flew too close to the sun. My wings caught fire and death is upon me.

Had awful dreams last night.

Awful dreams since the grief ceremony.
   That teacher's drumming has infiltrated my star journeying.

I dream of betrayal, sadness, pain and stuckness. I wake up and I slope off into the other room to type this entry. I want to face death alone. I *will* face death alone I guess. I am thinking of 2 ways I am scared of dying....

Choking and drowning. Both involve a fight.

I don't want to fight.
   I want to slip into it as if lured into some velvet-lined opium den.

Two of my students have been making art about drowning with turquoise sequins and cerulean blue watercolour.

I nearly drowned once....

I went down a fast river on a tyre in some remote place in Canada aged 15. I lost my group and my tyre. The current sucked me under and after a lot of splashing and gasping for air I went under and felt total peace. I knew my time was up.

A suspiciously Jesus-like man with a beard came from nowhere and scooped me out and promptly disappeared again.

I couldn't talk about it to anyone for a long time afterwards. I didn't think anyone would believe me. I remember shivering in my little bathing suit on the rivers edge.

A storm came at the same time and I just stood motionlessly in the rain. It was not only the summer I nearly drowned but also the first summer I really fell in love and it was totally unrequited.

In my heartbreak I sobbed constantly and listened to Alanis Morissette's *Jagged Little Pill* on my *Discman* on repeat.

I wished I had downed that summer of lost love.

Worse than drowning : Choking

My husband developed severe whooping cough in his 30's and would wake up terrified in the night unable to breathe.
   Desperate for air.
   We called three ambulances in one week. We stopped sleeping.
   And sat for hours and hours in A&E clutching shit instant coffees.

He's better now after 8 months of breathing difficulties at night.
   If someone so much as swallows a banana the wrong way in the staff room now I go into total terror. My body seizes up and I can't speak or move.
   Watching someone choke might actually be worse than choking.
   A shamanic healer once told me it had happened in my ancestral line.

Death is cruel and life can be even crueller.

* * *

- **What feels lifeless for you at the moment?**
- **What needs reviving?**
- **What relationships need to die?**
- **Draw with charcoal**
- **Lie in the dark**
- **Make a playlist for your own funeral**
- **Light a candle for all those you have lost**

DEATH

XIII

DEATH

15

Temperance

Mediation/Extremism

Colour is born of the interpenetration of light and dark.

–Sam Francis

The element that strikes me most in this card is the fact that she has a black wing and a white one. She contains both polarities of light and dark.

Half raven half dove.

Yesterday she cut out a raven and images of a girl beneath a lake. Submerged between worlds.

I am trying to mediate between these two worlds as they both make a grab for her.

The first of these worlds is the darkness. Drowning under the bathwater. We tore out a weave of white spindly spider webs.

This world of darkness and fear keeps her stuck. Floored. In bed all day.

Static and at times catatonic.

She is thus held half in death.

The light half of these worlds sounds like the better option I hear you say?

But with it comes the demands of a world that doesn't allow for her terror and grief to co-exist.

Her soul seeks a life devoid of any reliance on anything.

How can anyone be relied upon when their own self reliance is so utterly shattered. A mirror in a million shards of glass.

The underworld is more seductive. Here she can sleep all day. Be a non attender of all things. Live off the morsels of the black meat that the raven brings and hide from all colour.

On this card the angel of temperance pours two vials of vitriolic substances into a steaming cauldron. One liquid is white, the other red.

Each week I bring her red paint and the white feathers. Black tears pour forth.
   The violence she witnessed in her previous country is extreme and so is her angel.

* * *

- **Make a collage using only black and white**
- **Be held in the light**
- **Rest in quiet darkness**

- **Meditate**
- **Show up anytime**
- **Listen to your angels**

THE WONKY WOMAN'S GUIDE TO TAROT

16

The Devil

Sensuality/ Licentiousness

I am more afraid of those who are terrified of the devil than I am of the devil himself

-Saint Teresa of Avila

Three poems for the Devil:

Rage at 12.38am
   I am so angry and so tired
   Sick of always being the one to 'do the work'
   The endless healing and workshops and therapy
   Whilst the devil kicks back
   Feeling 'fine' just dandy
   Even the devils I love
   Whilst the women pick up the pieces
   Of disowned misogyny
   Again and again throughout history
   I feel so raw and rageful
   And dissapointed

I tried to talk to you tonight
  About the awful thing
  But your ears and eyes were so closed
  It was impossible
  You kickback
  The ivy is growing thick up this tower
  And I'm cutting my long hair
  You might fall
  You just assumed my tresses would hold you
  Your starting to wound me like the others before you did
  But I'm stronger now
  The endless affirmations worked
  I'm not afraid to cut my hair
  You're not a big bad wolf
  But a scared little boy
  I need a female devil for the second coming
  I need to be met
  And I'm tired of doing the rescuing all day
  Whilst you kick back with the others

* * *

Down day with The Devil

All you want is a day off all week
Then it comes and you have to face yourself
No masks
No distractions
No busyness to hide behind
Just me
I try to twist the day into various shapes of your temptation

THE DEVIL

* * *

<u>Devil in the sand</u>

Love told me you were out of bounds
   And that's because my bound-ries were so fixed
   I am bound to be bound to you
   Binding love
   A ribbon wrapped around a plastic devil in a sand box
   And buried deep
   I still hear you growl beneath me
   And pace
   Your sleek back twisting
   Moving back and forth
   Towards and Away
   I love you
   We are still bound

I am always there
   In every grit and grain
   And pore of pain
   I am bound
   To your dark heart

* * *

- What details of your life is the devil in?
- What feels hateful?

- **What are you tempted by?**
- **Who and what is toxic in your life?**

THE DEVIL

17

The Tower

Demolition/Destruction

The day I was born, my house burnt down; the day I left home, the Twin Towers burnt down; and I lived in a jungle in India at 15.

-Neon Hitch

A-tishoo, a-tishoo. We all fall down.

In the middle of a raging storm, amidst fears of pandemic in the town next to mine, this is an obvious card to pick.

Not only a storm.

When I woke up in York today the bus ticket system was down. So I got a free bus ride into town. Town was deserted. All the roads were closed. A woman had jumped off a roof.
   The Tower indeed.
   Amidst the road chaos I found a loose goose waddling along the road.

Hail came. Wind came.

THE TOWER

    My umbrella blew inside out.

I imagine the goose fucked off to somewhere warm or marshy.

Homeless men in doorways grinned at me as I struggled with my luggage, as everything got soaked through.

They know these problems well.
    With wet sleeping bags they nurse damp rolled up cigarettes.
    These guys have real tower shit going on.
    They haven't even got a tower to jump from.
    They have to die from addiction instead.

A woman in my choir fell from her balcony on the 4th floor. She almost died. Broke both knees. She was airlifted to hospital. The doctors couldn't believe she emerged alive.

As she fell into the abyss in slow motion on a dark rainy evening, she said that she had only one thought.

That thought was gratitude.

Thank God it was me and not my children – was her only thought.

Thank God.

Thank God.

She thanked God all the way down until she hit the concrete at the bottom. The doctors said: 'you've got some serious guardian angels'.
    'I know' she replied.

With the fall comes it's the ground that catches you.

* * *

- What chaos is coming up for you in life at the moment?
- Can you find your calm centre in the eye of the storm?
- What 3 things would you save from a fire?
- What in your life needs to fall/burn down?

THE TOWER

18

The Star

Openness/Denial

It is not in the stars to hold our destiny but in ourselves.

-William Shakespeare

This card always reminds me of my best friend.

She's an Aquarius, the water carrying sign this card is linked with.

It's her 36th birthday next week. I posted her a sexy, bright silk camisole and some love heart sweets.

Like the woman on the star card with her luscious curls loping around her low cut top, my dear friend is a bit of a lush.

Well she was. Before she became an exhausted mother of three precocious and wild children, one of whom has severe special needs.

She is a wonderful mother. She carried all three babes beautifully in her water carrying womb. She loves them unconditionally and lets them be who they are.

I know she'll give all her love heart sweets to them and let the youngest babe dribble on her sexy lingerie.

I see now, as the children grow, that she carries water in the form of tears that don't get let out. Tears that her babes will one day grow up and two of them at least will not need her so much.
    Tears that one of them will always need her. Especially as he grows up.

She has tears of lost love. Tears of who she was before being a mother stole the vessel of her previous body.

On the card, the starry wench pours blood on the lotus and water on the rose. The blood and mud of childbirth turns to beauty unfolding.

And the rose of grief grows towards the stars. The stars of each child's stressful birthday, each Christmas, each lost tooth and each frightened new threshold. All the times her son says no to a 'normal' child's life.

The biggest star is of course him, her son. Who is her sun. The brightest star there is.
    He shines on everything.

* * *

- **How can you shine?**
- **Who makes smile/ light up?**
- **Wish on a star**
- **How has life shaped you to be kinder?**

THE WONKY WOMAN'S GUIDE TO TAROT

19

The Moon

Mystery/Lunacy

Your madness fits in nicely with my own.

-Robert Wyatt

I love this lyric from his sea song.

Just been reading in the spiritual course I study that false insane thoughts spread more false insane thoughts and that real and loving thoughts cause more real love to spread.

I like this notion that what is false is insane.

I saw a Scooby Doo cartoon confirming that the media threatened Covid-19 virus was all just a hoax and that its just some silly guy under a sheet with eye holes.

All smoke and mirrors.

Scrappy dappy doooooooo.

What is real is sane.

I think of the times people have actually delivered. The mates that show up. The jobs that deliver. The people who come back. Who care. Who check in. Who stay.
   Who make tea and stir in a little extra sweetness without making a fuss.

The bread and butter people in our lives.

The staple friendships.

The kind dough that kneads our self esteem.

Often we pine after what and who is missing and don't celebrate what we have in our breast pockets or on our coffee tables.

This is the insanity

The moon is nearly full
   The waves outside my window seem charged and voluptuous
   Sensual
   Salty
   Todays its International Women's Day

There's a ripeness and a plumpness to the moons silver sheen

Spotlight on the feminine

The milk of stars

The swell of waves

I want to see only what's real and true

THE MOON

I want the false bride to resign so the true bride can step forth beneath the moonlight

Like a wet seal covered in the silk white lace of the surf

I want my lunacy to be as bright as her watery eye

Her heart under these waves
   Up high in the indigo sky

Within reach if I trust she rises from inside me
   Attached by a piece of string to my womb

Lunar queen
   Tears as she returns
   Always when I need her

Her full self

* * *

* * *

- **What is your madness?**
- **Who does it come out best with?**
- **What or who is mysterious to you?**
- **How can you flow with the great mystery?**
- **Look at the moon and speak to her.**

THE WONKY WOMAN'S GUIDE TO TAROT

XVIII

The MOON

20

The Sun

Energy/Giddiness

To correct a natural indifference I was placed half-way between misery and the sun. Misery kept me from believing that all was well under the sun, and the sun taught me that history wasn't everything.

-Albert Camus

Couldn't have picked a better card.

Today marks my 38th trip around the sun.

I feel like my heart might burst.
   I woke up to umpteen birthday messages which always makes me want to burst into tears. Then in the same glance I saw my sweet friend Benita has been affected by a huge and devastating family tragedy.
   I left her an incomprehensible sobbing voice mail. My heart feels so incredibly tender today.

I did my first Zoom call and felt exposed like a person under a bright dentist lamp.

Bunged some crap clothes on and headed to meet a friend for a Moroccan root vegetable tagine made by old town gods with a pot of rose infused coffee. Any excuse for rose coffee.

At 38 I give less of a fuck how I dress or what my unruly hair is doing. I barely put on make-up. Just a terracotta lip gloss that makes me feel earthy and tastes of cinnamon.

My friend plans edible headdresses for our local Jack in the Green festival in May.

Until yesterday May seemed a long way away with the endless February rain we've had. Months of grey cloud and puddles. Flood warnings and road resurfacing.

But today it's May in my heart.

I sip my Rose coffee and we giggle about various topics and discuss how grief so often partners with joy.

The banks of my heart are full to bursting as we mop up the last shared green lentil stew with warm pitta and I dash to meet meet my mum, sister and her three kids in a lurid, tacky ice-cream parlour. Kaspa's with a K.

The girls give me cards they have made with felt-tips and glitter. One has a vase of daffodils, the other an extravagant sundae.

Like the ones we attempt to eat. With electric blue and magenta turrets of ice-cream and rainbow sprinkles.

I feel totally sick but that's eclipsed by overwhelming love.

THE SUN

Charlotte has brought us both matching crystal beaded bracelets from the aquarium gift shop with her pocket money. She says if we wear them at the same time we are connected.

   She tells me about Baxter the lobster.

They hurry home after their ice creams and I feel the tears prick as I say goodbye. I linger with my hugs and smell the faint smell of bubble-gum ice cream on their soft hair.

Every half term they get more beautiful.

I have an hour before dance class and I feel my swollen heart is like the Sussex river banks. Major flooding is likely.

By the 4th track from the end on the dance floor I catch sight of my crystal bracelet. Tears stream not just from my cheeks but down my arms, neck, chin and chest.

My face more messy from crying than after the unicorn knickerbocker glory. I'm not sure I'll be able to stop.

I think of the girls' faces. My female lineage.
   How these times with my mother, sister and her daughters are deeply deeply precious moments that I will one day long for more than anything again.

I long for them even as they are unfolding. I ache with loving.

Even if the content is so sweet it's actually sickly.

The sun brought a year's worth of sentimental blessings in one day. With a flake 99 jammed in.

***

- **Who is the sunshine of your life?**
- **What brings you joy?**
- **What makes you Shine?**
- **When was the last time you felt really alive?**
- **Sit in the sun everyday**
- **Open the curtains**

THE SUN

21

Judgement

Revival/Evaluation

Good judgement comes from experience, and experience comes from bad judgment.

-Rita Mae Brown

Been doing a lot of writing around the subject of judgement and shame this week. Judgement breeds shame. Shame is guilt's older, bigger tougher brother.

I did a three day grief ceremony over the weekend and it wasn't sorrow and tears that I met, no.
   It was the other side of grief: guilt and shame.

I think we are all feeling this on some level, particularly amidst climate change fears disrupting even the fortunate western world.

Floods and fires. Pandemics.

Guilt using a plastic straw, burning sage, being vegetarian but still eating goats' cheese, using hand sanitiser, not using hand sanitiser, having a child.

Even oat milk's bad.

As I spoke to a random woman in H&M the other day, we both shared our massive guilt of even being in the shop and browsing the sale section.
   I felt slightly relieved and a little presence of love to even share this moment of confession with a total stranger who was feeling much the same.

We both admitted shopping has become a guilty secret.
   We chatted about how hard it is to make ethical choices at times and that the ethical section t-shirts looked a bit itchy and see through.

'Don't judge me me I normally only shop in charity shops', I declared.
'Stopping breathing is probably the most ethical choice', she joked.

We live in even more guilt in these times. Survivors guilt.
   Knowing our biosphere might not survive us.
   It's been helpful to recognise that guilt and shame are ways of grieving. Grieving our separation from love.
   Judgement is simply the effort to remain in a place of polarised opinion.

You are ok/You are not ok.
   You are good/You are bad.
   Your a Tory/You're a nice person
   You voted remain/You didn't
   You don't recycle/You cycle.
   You don't use sanitary towels/You have a smug hemp tote bag.

Judgement is damning and deathly, hence the cemetery where the naked couple stand. Makes me think of my teenage years where risk meant shagging someone in a cemetery. 'But what if an angel with a trumpet catches us?',

These days the stakes are higher.

Teens risk seeing species decline rapidly before they reach their sweet sixteenth, they risk adding to further plastic in our oceans by using condoms.

They risk their children (if they don't use condoms) facing a very uncertain future.
   They risk judgment not for dyeing their hair green but for using hair dye that contains water pollutants and pointless packaging.

They risk judgment not for having piercings but having piercing voices in protests that are shut down.

The world is fucked and cemetery sex is now cleaner than our sea water. Let's not judge our teenagers. We ruined more than their illegal raves.

* * *

- **Who are you being very judgmental of?**
- **Could you do a loving kindness meditation for the people you hate?**
- **Can you do a gestalt chair exercise and be in the mind of the opposing view to see their side?**
- **Let yourself off the hook**

JUDGEMENT

22

The World

Wholeness/Materialism

It isn't necessary to imagine the world ending in fire or ice. There are two other possibilities: one is paperwork, and the other is nostalgia.

-Frank Zappa

Yesterday I went into my therapy session with two masks I'd made.

The first was a fire mask. It had bull horns with red ribbons flowing from them and dried flowers sprouting from the horn tips. Dried as if burnt to husks.

In the centre of the forehead was a red and golden flower with a yellow shiny button at its centre denoting the sun.
   The eyes were covered in red and silver unblinking crystals and black marks that looked like scars from burns.

A skull and crossbones sits in the centre of the nose cavity suggesting a warning about fire breath from nostrils.

And finally a red sequin snake or dragon tongue slips out. I put this mask on and felt shame rise up in my cheeks.

The burn of embarrassment.

Who am I to wear this mask and express my fire? My power? I looked across at the other mask and felt debased.

The other mask was a frozen snow queen mask. Head covered in icicles and frost-covered leaves. Frozen tears stream down from the sharp gaze.

Ribbons covered in snowy owls suspended from the face. Two silver tusks hang down like swords.

When I put this mask on I feel cruel. The critic.

She is so cold. Her heart is frozen. No empathy or warmth.

She tries to put the fire out.

The owl's wisdom is suspended in shame. Wisdom is rejected. No life grows here.

Not even tears are shed.

As these two masks meet face to face I'm reminded of Norse mythology, from where fire and ice creation is born.

I feel both the lava and the compacted ice. Both burn me.

I spent three days with these masks in grief ceremony. Feeling the burn.

The shame that comes with grieving.

Who am I to be here? Why can't I cry? Why is my heart so fucking frozen?

I met my deadness.

My ancestral trauma.

The un-talked about child abuse.

Flashbacks of the times I played dead or took a risk and got severely burnt. I thought about my addictions.

Addiction to shame, which Robert Bly talks about. I'm starting to get what he means.

In this place the world is born from fire and ice.

I merged the masks in a drawing and saw the gatekeeper. The free child spirit.

An other worldly being.

The free child who wasn't shamed for raging or crying for what was intrinsically wrong with the world.

This spirit is dynamic, alive, comedic and playful.

This spirit contains the whole world and stands at the gateway to God. Grief is a gateway and shame is a sacred wound.

The world sits on fire and ice.

* * *

- **How do you take on the world?**
- **What does the world have to offer you?**
- **Who means the world to you?**
- **Can you seen the world in a grain of sand?**
- **What makes you world weary?**

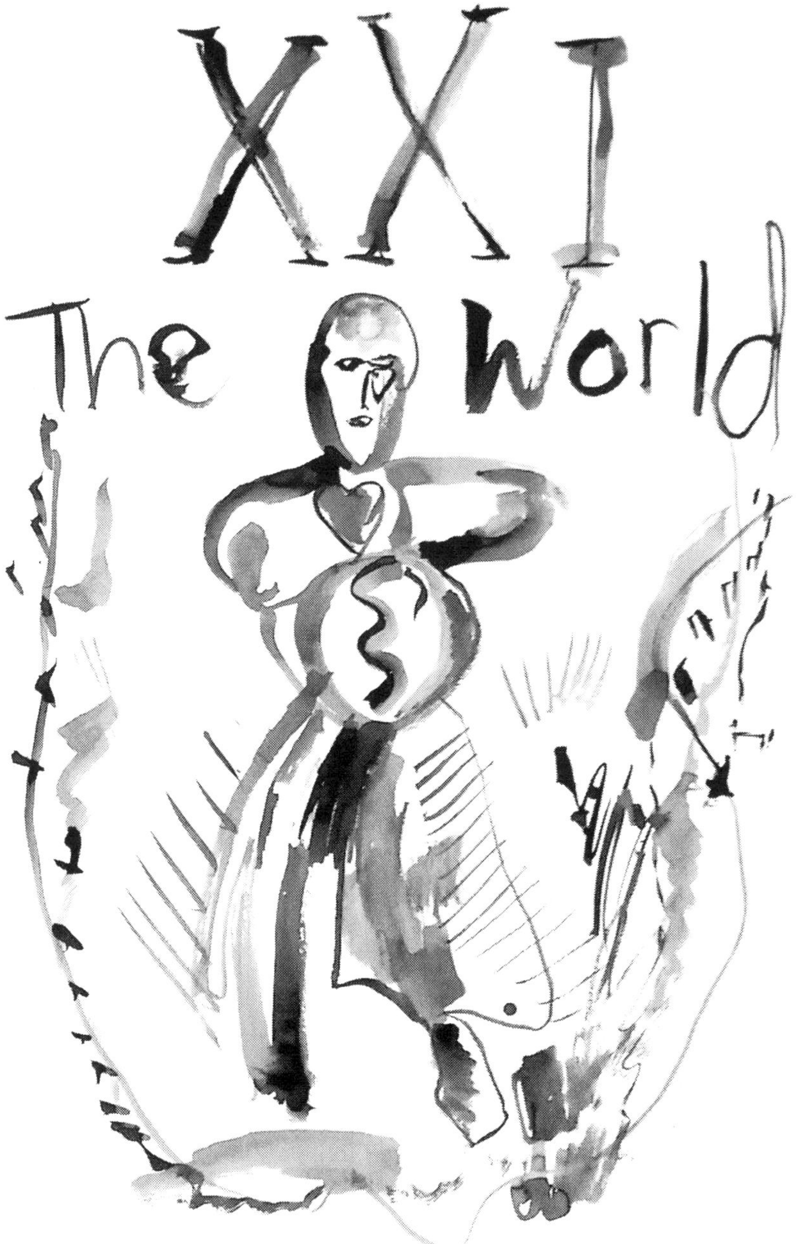
XXI
The World

23

Ace of Wands

Inspiration/Inflexibility

There is something about a closet that makes a skeleton terribly restless.

-Wilson Mizner

(An ode to Skeleton Woman and last nights dream)

Hearing the drum beat
   Feeling myself want want want

The wanting is almost unbearable
   The longing so painful
   A deep thirst
   A deep valley
   Wanting wanting wanting
   Hungry
   Starving

I need you inspiration
   I want you

I'm lost without my scratched baby, my wounded creator

She's not even my baby
   Abandoned by busyness
   The rest of her family is so busy no one even knows she's gone and has made her way into my arms

Soothing her clawed body

She crawled into my enclosed and lonely curtained off space

She's not even mine
   Not even fostered or adopted

Just borrowed like a library book with a due back date stamped violently all over her body in smudged blood ink

With a packet of Jaffa Cakes at my feet, a chalk drawing of an egg and a single blue flame

I am no longer in the dream.
   I have no baby and I am alone

School made me cut my nails
   I cannot scratch my body

I feel so abandoned

No baby to hold

Inflexible, impenetrable

I feel empty and alone

Home is a long way home

The ground is a long way off

On the 10th floor I look down at the specks of people floating past on an isolation seafront jolly

Masks out. Pace on.

Stay home.

I want Inspiration.

He feels like he's buggered off out for his daily walk too

Maybe to get more Jaffa Cakes

Loaves and fish got a bit stale and putrid

I want my baby

She's gone back to her busy awful family

Her wounds so open to infection

To dirt and dogs and that dusty old house

I want my baby

She is not here

Only my blue candle and my unhatched egg

* * *

- What inspires you?
- Poetry/art/ zoos/cooking/ crochet/horror films?
- How are you being inflexible?
- What stands in the way of your inspiration?
- Can you play with your own creative blocks?
- Who is the most inspiring/uninspiring person?
- How do you nurture your creative baby?
- Are you too busy for her?

Ace of Wands

24

2 of Wands

Choice/Misrepresentation

I've always been misrepresented. You know, I could dress in a clown costume and laugh with the happy people but they'd still say I'm a dark personality.

-Tim Burton

Taking back control.

Women have choices. Be a career woman and an earth mother. Breast feed for years. Own your body and get a flat stomach weeks after giving birth.

Run after work. Sprint with your pram. Join mother-and-baby groups, dress to kill. Put on that red lippy. Don't wear underwired bras. Use tummy control pants. Get bikini beach ready, home educate, meet your career goals, don't age.

Don't get fat
   Be more of who you are
   Be mindful
   Eat clean and green

Get slutty in the bedroom
I said, DON'T GET FAT
Don't age
Listen to your child
Always always have great hair
Fuck like it doesn't all hurt

Don't moan

Choices.

I sometimes feel misrepresented. Don't you?

* * *

- **Do you feel misrepresented?**
- **How can you speak on behalf of yourself?**
- **Is your voice being heard?**
- **How can you speak on behalf of others?**

2 OF WANDS

25

3 of Wands

Planning/Dogmatism

Dogmatism makes for scientific anaemia.

-Gordon W. Allport

It feels such a relief to write this morning
    I have horrific toothache. I can't eat solid food

Meant to be having a romantic dinner out with my husband tonight

First time eating out since Christmas
    I feel really tender and wobbly as I write

Toothache makes me feel really vulnerable and super sensitive

I have to abandon plans
    Which I hate

I am abandoning myself a lot

3 OF WANDS

Anna the Planner is often my joke title. I over plan. Over commit. Every inch of space in my life is taken up. Just like my mouth is taken up with teeth.

When one swells up in pain the whole mouth cannot cope

This is how it feels

I've crammed to many mouthfuls of what doesn't serve me

Too much sweetness
   Too much to chew on

I haven't done any of the teaching planning I was meant to do over the holiday

Last time I got toothache was when Triston and I had a holiday

It lasted for days and days there is such pressure to be who I am not in the school holidays
   Why can't I just be myself in the day job. I cannot.

There are rules. I can't be myself. My self isn't unacceptable
   To me especially

So I wait till the holidays and I feel the ache of longing
   Belonging
   is to *be longing* for all that is longed for

on the opposite side of the ice rink
   beneath the ice- my wild twin
   All that I am not

come to work with me

* * *

- **How do you over plan?**
- **How do you over commit?**
- **What would it be like to take your weekend self to work and working self to your weekend?**
- **How can you be more spontaneous?**
- **More flexible?**
- **More wild?**

3 OF WANDS

26

4 of Wands

Achievement/Sameness

There's a kind of numbness, a sameness, a lack of motivation in 'good job' culture.

-J. K. Simmons

Cheese and pickle sandwich please.

Kids who order the same lunch from the canteen each day.

Images of the Fall and Rise of Reginald Perrin, a 70's sitcom.

Sick of his marriage, his family and the daily grind of his job, Reginald Perrin comes up with the only logical solution for such a deep midlife crisis: He fakes his own death. After various attempts at creating a new life, Reginald adopts a disguise and returns to his old life to find that nothing much has changed. He even re-marries his wife, Elizabeth, after wooing her at his funeral, and he gets a job at his former company, where he manages his own memorial fund.

4 OF WANDS

I think life moves in patterns. It can feel like a circle and a daily grind but actually it's a spiral bringing us closer towards our centre. Our true essence.

The cheese and pickle of our true hearts.

Our Sunshine Desserts.

I didn't get where I am today without going round in a million circles.

*　*　*

- **How has life got boring and monotonous?**
- **How do you put yourself in a box?**
- **How has the mundane become boring?**
- **What do you feel you are achieving day to to day?**
- **How are you playing the role of yourself in your own life?**

4 WANDS

27

5 of Wands

Confrontation/ Strife

Most of us are dragged
towards wholeness.
We do not understand the breakdown of what has gone before.
We do not understand.
We cling to the familiar,
Refuse to make necessary sacrifices,
Refuse to give up habitual lives,
Resist our growth.
We do not understand rebirth,
Do not accept the initiation rites.
Most of us are dragged
Towards wholeness.

-Marion Woodman

Five weeks into lockdown I got desperate and made a self employed artist vision .

Confronted with myself and my aging womb

Childless and nearly 40

In the top right hand corner I cut out a stamp sized square of a place called 'the Mole Man house.'

Amidst a whole load of other gumph.

On Monday during my phone therapy session (because of lockdown) I watched a builder tip a wheelbarrow's worth of rubble off the cliff edge behind my house

'Chuck that shit out' my therapist said,
   As if on cue after I shared that I am either too much or not enough for everyone.
   Trouble and strife.

But wait - the half-built building opposite
   I'd never noticed it before

Hang on I thought,
   It looks like that tiny square of the Mole Man's house.

Indeed it did

After hanging up the phone I dug out the magazine I found it in

There it was: 'the Mole Man house', bought by an artist whose life I fell in love with

Triumphant and pregnant at 52 and making wild art about her teenage years

I thought of my own concreted tunnels
   Derelict places

5 OF WANDS

Abandoned mental asylums broken into as a teenager

People I know right now in lockdown living in one

Time stopping.....
   Sanatogen haze
   Smashed up ballrooms
   Medication cards
   Beautiful 24 year olds shitting on the middle of the floor in protest

I thought of your cat
   Your black kohl eyes
   Your beautiful bump
   Your adidas flip flops
   The black and white and white and black bathroom tiles

Your punch bag

Leather jackets full of studded poetry

All the times I've given up on being an artist

The times I let myself be life's punch bag
   Life and strife dictated

And then there you were rebuilding my idea

Its never too late
   To be an eternal teenager
   To miss out on those years and be part of them at the same time
   I put on some tunes

The tunnels may be filled with concrete but they are still there

In lockdown your black baby waits to come through fallopian tubes
  These are not blocked

But alive and well and living in a mole hole in Hackney

Confronting life.

* * *

- **What strife takes you off your path?**
- **What events or decisions are very confronting for you?**
- **What can't you face?**
- **Who can't you face**
- **What needs digging up?**
- **What tunnels need filling in?**

5 OF WANDS

28

6 of Wands

Victory/Pridefulness

The struggle goes on. The victory is in the struggle, for me. And I accepted that a long time ago.

-Al Lewis

I sit in the art therapy centre waiting for the next child to fill the collaged butterfly walls with sad lockdown tales

Alcoholic parents, no siblings to play with, planets of rage without a universe to exist

How much *Plants vs Zombies* on Xbox can be played
    or downloadable colouring sheets for four straight months

Before these kids forget their times tables, their manners and their minds

Like me, the adult who scrolls endlessly on Facebook looking for power smoothie powder, and mindful mantras

Buying cheap shoes for expensive dollars from Malaysia with foam flip flop soles that come in plastic packets that take 4 months to deliver made by women in a factory whose knees ache

I do not have the energy to demand a refund or send them back

I can't even wear these foam clown shoes indoors

They are a hideous reminder of my dented pride

The part of me that craves anything to quench the voice that tells me I'm nothing and that my dreams aren't real

I'm shit

Then just as I'm on the precipice of the void something else calls

A new devil in disguise worse than the Facebook advert Malaysian factory shoes

This devil: Ambition and Victory

It calls me from this wounded place with promises of artistic projects, commissions, conversations, timetables, to do lists, zoom meetings, Facebook lives

My CV can get as bloated as the joints behind me knees currently are

I can be somebody

Somebodies don't get lonely

Except when they do

They are always on that precipice of being a nobody

Always faltering on the edge of that existential cliff

Trying to cling on to their somebody with good shoes for dear life

I'm someone with sturdier shoes surely?

The backs of my knees creak and ache

I can't hold myself up anymore

Remembering live interviews, commissions, watches, likes, smiley heart emojis from people you never met in real life

When you walked into a room
    Or stole a party
    Turning heads and limbs and ears

Like mutilated corkscrews

Corkscrewing yourself into a someone

Into a shape that others could identify
    And possibly want to walk through

The shapes of past achievements, accolades, trophies

Worn out badges of honour

They weigh so much

Maybe its ok to not know your seven times table

6 OF WANDS

To have a masters in mindful colouring

Maybe its OK to not get up in the morning or wash yourself or the three day old dinner plates that sit where you left them

Maybe its OK to have knees that feel 100 years older than they are

Victory and Failure
    Are devil twins

Grabbing at our swollen ankles
    Deep vein thrombosis

I am now starting to think that all the someone's are stranded by their own success and are my inescapably alone

Whilst the no ones are in good company

Living like they don't matter
    In flip flop shoes.

* * *

- **What are your victories?**
- **What are your struggles?**
- **How do you feel defeated?**
- **When was the last time you felt victorious?**

THE WONKY WOMAN'S GUIDE TO TAROT

VI 6 of WANDS

29

7 of Wands

Resolve/Defensiveness

I do have a vulnerable side. I think a lot of people have a misperception of me. They only see the tough, defensive, aggressive side. But every woman is vulnerable.

-Rihanna

I don't want to be a comedian anyway I thought to myself. My husband had said to listen to funny stuff.

One woman made endless jokes about her sex life. How she doesn't need alcohol to be a slut.

YAWN.

My favourite jokes were about shoes.

One guy lost his shoes during a hot yoga class. That in itself was slightly funny.

I liked the one who said she dreamt that her 30's would involve kicking off slingbacks and removing one earring to talk on the phone. She imagined she would have an American accent.

Not because she was American but because she was so confident.

It reminded me of imagining myself as an adult when I was young. Similarly, I also just imagined the older I got, the danglier my earrings would get and the more permed my hair would be (I was an 80's kid).

I imagined that I would be the sort of person who would wear red lipstick in bed and I would be Australian (because I loved Neighbours and Home and Away).

I would have a boyfriend called Scott and work in a surf café.

My resolve never paid off. I don't have my ears pierced, look good in a swimsuit or wrestle with dingoes.

But I could whip up a great smoothie for a beach hunk at a moments notice. Thank god NutriBullets were invented.

Defensive yes. I don't want to follow my dreams anyway. Those dreams will simply curl into the perm that never was.
G'day mate.

***

- **What are you being defensive about?**
- **Do you use sarcasm often?**
- **When was the last time you allowed yourself to be vulnerable?**
- **How can you resolve to be more open about your flaws and fuck ups?**
- **Can you laugh at yourself?**

7 OF WANDS

30

8 of Wands

Responsiveness/ Reactions

I envy the people who say, 'oh, well, I've got my name in the golden book and I'm going to be entered into the pearly gates.'

-William Shatner

BOOM! This card is that.
    A meteorite landing out of the cosmos! A rainbow appearing out of the blue!
    A golden gate of opportunity! All the exclamation marks!!!!!!!!
    I welcome this card with open arms.

Today is a day out of the blue. I'm off sick with flu. So I have a golden gated opportunity to write from my pool of tissues with tiger balm scented finger tips and snot filled sinuses.

I cannot move easily but I can write freely.

Although worryingly the gate in the image looks more shut than open.

The rainbow's on the other side and I'm stuck on the side of the meteorite missile. More apocalypse than rainbow pool party.

Lately I have been missing some golden opportunities. More due to exhaustion than anything else. Tomorrow night I will miss the spoken word night where I hoped to share a couple of these entries.

Maybe they, or I, am not ready. Although I did have a great gold outfit planned. I always miss the good job adverts, the fastest trains, the best holiday deals.

I know all the wrong people. And have the professional networking confidence of a bat with only one wing.

Lopsided luck.

My rainbow is always half full, never mind my glass.

Today's meditation mantra from my little meditation book 'I am not a victim of the world!' Extra exclamation mark!

It's hard not to feel a victim of the world when the world pits us against one another in a massive game of human bulldog.

I found myself Googling successful people I used to be mates with earlier. Before they got...successful.

Perfect way to self-sabotage the day (when you already have flu and are wearing worst baggy kneed pyjamas).

My golden threshold has opened a crack and then slammed many times like a broken security gate.

It's a celebrities house I'm stalking. Not mine.

Maybe one day I'll return to my planet, where the meteor is from. Maybe there you don't need a CV or references.

* * *

- What opportunities await you?
- What golden gate could you walk through?
- Google yourself. Do you like what's there? If not what would you like to be known for?
- Does your CV reflect your creative dreams?
- Start a blog/YouTube channel/newsletter/zine about something you love

8 WANDS

31

9 of Wands

Persistence/Martyrdom

I am selfless only to an extent, I can't be a martyr, I have a daughter to raise.

-Mukul Dev

One third of the way through the tarot deck. At this juncture persistence is necessary. It's getting harder. But I'm 'good' so I'll do it if I said I would. Resent resent resent.

I often think about the martyr archetype.

A friend of mine's been working with hers. Drawn in wonderful green and red chalks. Seething rage and jealousy steaming off her anxiety ridden halo.

A chalk dust smile. Easily erased.

Mine's always been pretty obvious. I learned from an early age to be the good girl when my devilish sister bunked school and had grass stained knees.

Mine were milky white and I did all my dull history homework about agricultural laws. Learned to be nice and stay nice:

Now
  I'm
  Closing
  Everything

Being nice meant I closed all the other parts of me up. Zip.
    Anything not nice was deemed unacceptable. So I bitched and hid from myself.
    Sent unkind notes across the classroom regarding my own persona.

I've recently had a real revelation in a fairly new, emerging friendship.
    We don't do phone calls or coffee dates, we just leave each other lengthy stream of consciousness monologue voice mails. Whatever our mood.

We've decided it's better that way.

We take the time to really hear the other without interrupting the flow. No one hogs the conversation.
    No one feels they have to please the other. No fake interested noises.
    Unlike other friendships we're sharing deeply and personally straight away. Why? Because we feel heard.
    We're not martyrs to each other. We just keep talking and make space to listen. Zero interruption;
    Or pleasing.

It's deeper listening when you can't see. You have to look with your ears and hear with your eyes.

I spent my 20s rebelling dangerously to counteract my martyr. I've tried many times to banish her to some attic but she persists. She's the one who would kick me when I was hungover. 10 hail Mary's you drunken whore!

She's an enabler.

She's well immersed in a drama triangle of her own making.

She looks innocent. But she's not. She's so punishing it hurts. But she also needs to be honoured. Transfigured even.
   I think of stigmata. The wounds on her open palms. Receiving so much contact that it is wounding. Giving so much self judgment the cuts re-open.

I too have over given in recent years.
   Feeling lately its time to take something back.

Focusing more on being an artist than just an art therapist.. fulfilling my own creative holes instead of just plugging those of others.

My martyr needs some forbidden fruit. Pomegranate seed stains on her magnolia feathers. My martyr needs Forgiveness.
   With a big F'ing red juicy F.

* * *

- **What are you being a martyr about?**
- **Who and what do you resent?**
- **What are you sacrificing for a role in your life?**
- **Do something naughty/badass**
- **Get into trouble**

9 OF WANDS

•

32

10 of Wands

Tenacity/Exhaustion

Here are a few verses from my newly discovered favourite poem from Mark Nepo....

She still smells the womb-sea and I,
  the rocks of this world. She's eager
  to be here, though her eyes don't under-
  stand the many shades of weight.

But I feel compelled to translate weights
  which means I sense the things
  that hide in wood and stone,
  the things that boil in the pot
  of human traffic.

How I make hymns of my father's pain.
  How my friend's little girl will make
  portraits of how I burn.
  This is necessary. It's
  how spirit recycles.

Today my 90 year old father showed me two beautiful salt and pepper pots made of cut glass that were a wedding present for his parents in 1923.

Its his only possession from them

I find them very beautiful but they carry a kind of weight and deep fragility

Our lives are a series of handed down salt and Pepper pots

Often they are made of glass

We carry the weight if these pots and gifts of glass, wood and stone

The weight of our ancestry and our lineage

It chinks along with our DNA in the spirits recycling bank

Sprinkling onto our days like salt and pepper, flavouring our perception

I heard some one say: it's not what we carry but how we carry it

Maybe that is where the term 'a pinch of salt' came from

That the weight of the world could be carried with a pinch of that womb sea salt

* * *

- **What weight are you carrying?**
- **How can you yield without collapsing?**
- **What do you carry forth?**
- **What needs dropping?**

10 OF WANDS

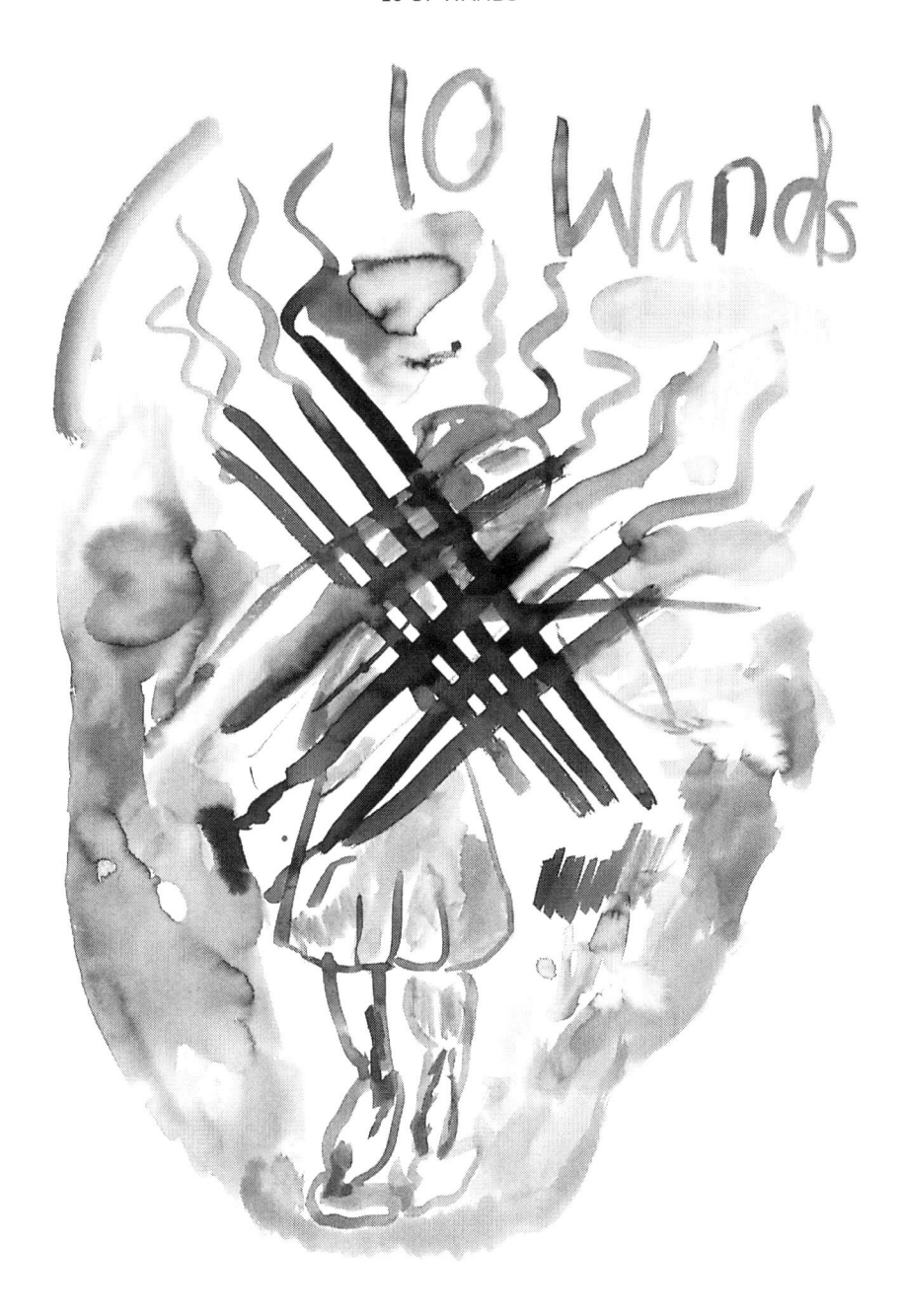

33

Knave of Wands

Enthusiasm /Inexperience

In the realm of ideas everything depends on enthusiasm... in the real world all rests on perseverance.

-Johann Wolfgang von Goethe

She is the bounding sister of last night's Knight of Wands with his bravado up his armoured arse. She is the carefree sibling. Skipping naked. Wands out.

My enthusiasm to write and to be a bit comedic is backfiring. I am totally inexperienced in the world of humour.

After all, as my supervisor says, all I do is read about trauma recovery and zen meditation.

I don't tend to go and see stand-up. Too busy raking through old wounds using tapping. Or affirming my worthiness through breath-work whilst swearing under my breath.

Laughter? That's for funny people. Not me. Therapists don't have a great deal of humour. Serious business.

Even my inner child stops herself sniggering by putting a hand over her sweet mouth.

But maybe, just maybe, humour isn't something we learn but something that we innately have, like a birthmark or an elbow.

Maybe inexperience is ok.

And maybe all I need is enthusiasm. **'Enthusinexperience'** my new buzzword.

Definition: enthusiastically unprepared.

Maybe if we knew what we were in for we would never have signed up.

With a red feather in her hat, a cape (surely in a cape we can do *anything*) and not much else (I don't think she even has pants on- in this card) - off she goes.

No map just her excitement and her golden Instagram fans.

* * *

- **What are you enthusiastic about?**
- **Make a cape**
- **Wear it**
- **Put the work in**
- **Let your idea fly**

THE WONKY WOMAN'S GUIDE TO TAROT

34

Knight of Wands

Bravado/Strength

I've got a friend who is a lion tamer. He used to be a school teacher till he lost his nerve.

-Les Dawson

Melancholy I could do, but bravado and strength?

I guess the part I can relate most to is the image of the lion.

How we put on a brave face. Bravery is a weird one for me. I'm not sure that strength is the same as bravery.

I know brave people who are not strong and strong people who are not brave. Bravery is a face. Strength comes from the body.
   Some of the bravest faces I know are crumbling inside. I can think of crumbling bodies like my Grandmother's that were so strong.

Her arms carried me even after she died.

One of my favourite mantras from a Course in Miracles is 'In my defence-lessness, my safety lies'. I have wrestled with this statement over and over.
In the end I come back to Aslan on the stone table. Dying for love.

I want to drop down all weapons, come off my high horse and lay down with the lions.

Golden heart.
Blood sacrifice.

I think of the girl who paints her grief stricken face each day with don't fuck with me make-up. I think of the boy who puffs out his robin chest before buckling at the knees.
What we need is heart medicine. Four-chambered alchemy

Raw roar.

**

- **How have you been brave in the face of fear?**
- **What have you sacrificed for love?**
- **What weapons could you lay down?**
- **Who is your warrior teacher?**

KNIGHT OF WANDS

35

Queen of Wands

Attention/Distraction

I love who I am and I love my life, but if I could be someone else, I'd be Beyoncé in two seconds.

-Dakota Fanning

This card is all about calling forth attention in productive ways. It's a strong feminine kick arse card.

One that I really need today (I couldn't feel further from it).
  This card is creative, dynamic and wonderfully constructive. Think Vogue editor Anna Wintour or someone like actress Helen Mirren or artist Lizzo.

Self confident.

Knows what she wants and, more importantly, does *not* want and can get shit done in creative ways just by being her sexy damn self.

She really is here to fight the patriarchy. She doesn't get what she wants by acting like a dude. On the contrary, she uses her feminine artistry and intuition and doesn't always need to put on heels or shoulder pads.

She loves herself. She owns her body and she works with what she has.

I quite often try to inhabit this character but it's highly unsustainable.

I even once wrote an entire women's voice speech channelled through this archetype.
   You see the Queen of Wands doesn't need to become empowered, she already is. Simply by being her self.

I was going to drop the word authentic in here but I've grown to slightly loathe this term. If we have to try to be authentic we are probably *not* being authentic.

Authenticity is for those who probably don't use that word on a regular basis.

They are too busy keeping it real.
   Queen of Wands is pure sass and conviction.

As I write I am sitting in yellow 'who gives a fuck about my cellulite' hot pants and hoodie that says 'she who dares wins'. In a minute I will put on my frumpy teacher clothes with a knee length hem, perhaps even a hair bun and some form of buttoned up cardigan or blouse.
   I will go out into the world and no one will see my yellow hot pant self.

Which is a shame because that version of me is better. She's lazier yes, but much more easy to be around. She's less uptight and softer around the edges.

She did a vision map in pyjamas yesterday. The day before she drank tea and left sweet rambling voicemails to girlfriends. Sometimes she just has a cry and eats chocolate whilst bleeding.

The shadow side of this Queen is distraction. She can self sabotage easily.
The confidence to go out in the word with her arse hanging out can backfire.

She is prone to internet trolls, misogynist gunfire from both men and other blouse wearing women.

She puts her neck on the line simply for owning her sexuality and using it as a creative force. For many years I was frightened of her.

As were the men.

This fear gets translated as hatred.

She represents all women at heart and often holds what men really want, if they were able to admit/recognize it.

Superwoman.

Of course she doesn't really exist. She's idealized. No woman can be a career whiz, mother of three, sex kitten, wife, artist and body builder. But that seems to be what Instagram expects of us.

It doesn't hurt to tap into her occasionally even when we are just at home in baggy jammies with a hot water bottle.

* * *

- **Are you owning it in the world?**
- **How are you going to fight the patriarchy today?**
- **Wear something sexy-frumpy**
- **Strut**

QUEEN OF WANDS

36

King of Wands

Direction/Suppression

The good life is a process, not a state of being. It is a direction not a destination.

-Carl Rogers

I spent yesterday with my dad in his local, The Tiger Inn.

We don't talk about politics. He writes satirical poems that sometimes get published in The Spectator. He has a hand written letter from Boris in a drawer. He was friends with the late millionaire Steward Wheeler who had dealings with UKIP.

He was telling me yesterday about Wheeler's infamous parties, where he hired out the whole of the London Dungeon for a dinner party and another time where he had buffets from every single country represented in culinary delights and full West Indian steel band.

Seems strange for someone who wants to keep England as a small toffee-nosed Island without migrants bringing their rich cultures. This England that, in my opinion, has got too big for its boots and needs to pipe down and sit at the back.

He argues at length with his labour supporter friend Ian at the pub.

I stay quiet.

Our relationship is fraught enough with many fissures. No need for politics to be another one. It probably would measure too high on the Richter scale and there would be no going back.

Our relationship would not withstand the weight.

My Dad loves a rags to riches story and Stewart grew up in an orphanage with a club foot. He was adopted by a rich couple and shipped off to Eton where he was mercilessly bullied and branded a cripple.

My father's background and education was not much different except he didn't have any money. He used an outdoor toilet.

He didn't go to Eton but was taught by Jesuit priests and played cricket.

He knows facts about pretty much everything and spent his whole life working for Customs and Excise.

Back in the day when careers were for life.

The King of Wands is a careers for life kind of man, he's a bit of a jobsworth and is *always* right.

Their an air of pompous righteousness but at the same time he's pretty fair and likes a good debate on question time.

There is an interesting depiction of a gecko or lizard on his robe.

This reminds me of my partner Triston.

The opposite of my dad he would be happy with a universal income and a European passport.

When Triston and I first met on Tinder he had created a backdrop on his profile picture using a hippy sarong tie dyed with red and black geckos on.

It could well have been a King of Wands cape.

Triston is logical, intelligent and fair. He has worked diligently in one job with no sick days since we met. All the best Wand King characteristics.

With a tiny slither of dancing gecko wild abandon on the weekends.

Lizards are for life, not just for Christmas.

* * *

- Who is your dictator?
- What direction does he bid you go in?
- Who's side are you on?
- Where is your slither of rule breaking wild abandon that doesn't follow the rules?

KING OF WANDS

37

Ace of Cups

Refreshment/Inundation

Love is the greatest refreshment in life.

-Pablo Picasso

This card is rather beautiful. Perhaps even my favourite

I have an interest in creative mysticism and this card incorporates just that

The idea that we are love. We each contain God

The presence of love never leaves us but we forget this

This card is a reminder of your guardian angel. The one who travels with you

It may even be your daemon

The part of us that takes the risk, volunteers to be the scapegoat, takes the blame, runs the gauntlet, integrates the shadow

ACE OF CUPS

The good cop and the bad cop

The bitter and the sweet

To me the Ace of Cups integrates this

Spirit turns to matter and matter is magic

A toast to our still small voice

Where Demons kiss Angels and Heaven lands on Earth

* * *

- **What does your still, small voice say?**
- **What refreshes your soul and spirit?**
- **Make some art**
- **Arrange some fresh flowers**
- **Find inner quiet in nature**

THE WONKY WOMAN'S GUIDE TO TAROT

ACE OF CUPS

38

2 of Cups

Attraction/Codependency

There are almost as many definitions of co-dependency as there are experiences that represent it.

-Melody Beattie

This card contains a real sweetness
   Two people gaze at one another
   Toasting the present moment
   Fountains of lions and dragonfish gush behind them. A lotus of love marks the spot as their cups clink

I refused a real wedding
   With the imposed vows
   I wanted to write my own and create my own ceremony with my beloved. Based on our own needs

My husband wore a powder blue velvet waistcoat and got a sharp haircut whilst I rocked up in a charity shop dress covered in Victorian flowers

We read a poem by the ancient mystic Hafiz and used Oriah Mountain Dreamer's 'The Invitation' as our vows: 'To be prepared to betray another, so's not to betray your own soul'

    I will not betray my own soul for marriage like so many other women in my family have done. We are very happy to live together but separate. Hand-fasted but not married

    Free range but not caged

    There is a steady flow of love between us, but it comes not just from one another. We have other fountains on the go

    Other tributaries

Because codependent love has almost killed me from heartbreak in the past. The Course in Miracles warns about 'relationships made special'

    If we put people on a pedestal they can only disappoint us

    We need to recognize the love that is all around us

    From nature, the environment, our cats, our enemies, our communities, our ancestors

    Not just the Milk Tray givers and takers. We are all part of love

    Even the abandoned and exiled ones

Especially them

Does anyone have a reason why these two should not been joined in matrimony? So say I

The lotus grows from mud.
    As do our hearts

Muddy relationships bring love
    I never washed the mud and grass stains off my wedding dress

* * *

- Who are you dependent on?
- Do you rely on one person to meet your needs?
- What gesture of independence could you make today?
- How can you rely on you more?

THE WONKY WOMAN'S GUIDE TO TAROT

39

3 of Cups

Celebration/Mania

Come and crush a cup of wine!

-William Shakespeare, Romeo + Juliet
   Act 1, Scene 2

Three women cavort. They've either had barrels of Aldi's cheap Spanish red or are at a Woodstock take over on a fuck ton of purple acid.

Having read Joan Dideon's ' Slouching towards Bethlehem ' and Olivia Laing's ' The Lonely City' over lockdown, I realised i was hungry for a 1960's style revolution.

Since the economic crash in 2008 and up until now there has been a 50's austerity vibe.

The Tories have been in power for ages and I now can't even order classmates own brand glue sticks for children at school because of budget cuts. I'm also really done with exposed light bulb décor and scaffold plank tables in restaurants.

Months of lockdown have brought a deep longing in me for social change.

Going to my friends 'The Spirit of Woodstock' show that was sanctioned by Brighton and Hove council to go ahead, despite the new 6 people restrictions felt, in itself, like a rebellious act.

you know like…
   Fumbling to put your seatbelt on after the beepy thing starts
   Sneaking the last red jelly baby
   Wearing yellow knickers at a funeral
   Painting your study purple
   Showing a bit of shoulder

His was a one man show about a festival.
   Rebel rebel.

Why?

Because this has been a summer in which no festivals took place. And no one was allowed near anyone without a vat of hand sanitiser and a plastic visor .

If 1969 was the summer of love

2020 was the Summer of Social distancing. Where love and touch was a distant memory.

Stay 2 meters apart it says on the roads that we walk on with our toddlers and dogs.

In this 2 hour show my friend took me through moon landings, riots and bad acid trips.

It made me long for pink onesies at Secret Garden Party festival, rose petal confetti at a wedding, invites taped to the fridge, tickets to gigs, wearing tiaras for the fuck of it, in a naff photobooth sporting face paint and an electric blue wig.

These things have been absent. Just Facebook arguments and shoddy Zoom yoga sessions where I might just turn my camera off and eat a Twirl behind the sofa.

This play was as much political as it was psychedelic.
    Exposing the naivety and vulnerability of the kids who lost their way in the aftermath of the Vietnam war. Where PTSD didn't have a name yet.

I guess the ways I partied hard in my 20's did leave me fairly broken and unable to drink rosé wine or cider again.

For me this play was a reminder that with great social change their are a lot of casualties and well as celebrations. Even if it's just loss of innocence.

I wonder what the aftermath of Covid will bring. Two-for-one vaccine shots?

Masked raves?

Online festivals? -Oh they already happened and were just irritating on a screen (clearly not fucked in a field enough).

As the Black Lives Matter protests have come to the forefront of our minds these last months, I felt a renewed hope on a balmy, yet slightly chilly evening, in St Ann's Well Gardens, where this play was performed.

The theatre industry is being called to go completely lo-fi and this solo production was a triumphant effort of bringing people together in coned bubbles with picnic blankets and less dope.

But NOT on a screen.

Wine in thermos*

*　*　*

- **What are you celebrating?**
- **What are you not celebrating?**
- **When was the last time you had a good night out?**
- **Get dressed up and pour Champagne in fancy glasses for the hell of it.**

3 OF CUPS

40

4 of Cups

Boredom/Satiation

I can excuse everything but boredom. Boring people don't have to stay that way.

-Hedy Lamarr

This is a good one for today. An ill day. I lay restlessly in bed. Feeling really grumpy and fed up. I have a much needed day to myself but I've had to sit with my pre-menstrual Medusa emotions. Restlessness turning to stone boredom.

   Bored of my job
   Bored of who I am in relationships
   Bored of emails and paperwork
   Bored of people pleasing
   Bored of being a constant disappointment to myself
   Bored of procrastinating
   Bored of fear
   Bored of hearing the same stories from myself and others
   Bored of social media
   Bored of spirituality and self help

But most of all, bored of endless tasks that don't seem to make anything change

What satiates me?
　I will make a list from today:

Watching 80's film Clash of the Titans in bed writing
　Writing some more
　E-mails from Dave and Andrew
　Tarot
　Bed
　Lemon and honey Eucalyptus oil
　My husband making me perfectly percolated coffee (this is the best moment in any day)
　Chocolate cake
　Ruby gem essence drops from Findhorn
　Cough syrup
　Reading my daily mediation
　Replying to Phoebe about her new children's book
　Radiators on all day (this rarely happens)

I always know I'm satiated when I don't look at my phone all day.

Most of these pleasures revolve around art, senses or friendships. None of them revolve around work, money or newsfeeds.

My work is often fulfilling but often that simple joy gets weighed down just by the sheer amount of it I have to do and then evaluate the fuck out of afterwards in Excel spreadsheets.

If only we could live more from the senses. From connection and creativity.

Not feedback forms and Fuckbook — I mean Facefuck — I mean Facefuckbookprick.

Ahhhhhhhhh.

I've lost my bloody phone. I'm cold turkey like a twitchy tech junkie.

It's horrid when you have to go crawling back to your old cracked screen phone in the drawer. Like smoking a used cigarette butt.

You know you shouldn't but you've not watched Youtube videos of your horoscopes all week.

If only boredom was more than a screen saver.

* * *

- **Who bores you?**
- **What boring routines are you stuck in?**
- **Change them up and add some spice.**
- **Make a list of things to do if you get bored.**
- **Do them.**

4 OF CUPS

41

5 of Cups

Regret/Despair

There's no such thing as perfect writing, just like there's no such thing as perfect despair.

-Haruki Murakami

How can I say yes to this card?
   Welcome regret and despair?

This is what is being asked of us during these times,

'Hello regret'

I regret not ever realising the pleasure of what it was to be in a room with people I liked or didn't like for that matter.

Being in a room with anyone was actually a privilege.

For not realising group gatherings may not always be possible.

For not realising that hope will sometimes slip through my fingers like the pink soap that I repeatedly wash my hands with.

That handwashing videos would become a thing and I would watch them staring at a screen, blank eyed.

I regret not showing people I loved them with touch enough.

That I didn't linger longer into hugs to smell the necks of those that I could make a nest in.

I regret signing up to so much bullshit.
   Giving my email to so many companies who don't matter.
   And not giving my email to so many who do.

I regret not staying in touch.

Hello despair.

I despair at having to wait in for food deliveries because I'm too terrified to go outside.

I despair at how many beautiful clothes I've stopped wearing only to don the same crap jogging bottoms and oversized cardigans day in day out.

Its Frock-off Friday tomorrow and I'm going to look fucking hot.

Its a defiant Facebook group I joined in an effort to conserve some personal dignity in a time where I might just die in yesterdays underwear.

No, I shall wear lipstick and straighten my overgrown fringe.

Heck I might even shave my armpits.

No, no need to go too overboard.

Fuck it! I will even wear a bra!

I've almost forgotten how to wear one.

Seeing DIY you tube videos about how to turn bras into masks.

My bras are probably too awful. Wonky underwiring and faded lace trims. And my cup size is probably not adequate to cover the rage my mouth wants to shout about.

Fuck you Boris screamed through a spongy wired ellipse from Primark essentials range.

I wonder if, when this is over, (if this is ever over) whether it will be like the 60's again and people will start fucking in the streets.

Naked Asda trips and LSD delivered by Ocado.
   All the shop workers will have died out.
   Or quit.

I don't suppose women will burn their bras. Too busy using them to catapult shit at their husbands and precious children they've been forced to stay home with.

A great way of dealing with extraneous faecal matter when the loo roll finally runs out.

'No Tobias I can't teach you conjunctions or decimal fractions, Mummy's got day wine to drink.'

Regret and despair are everywhere and we are forced to invite them to dinner.

5 OF CUPS

A dinner of out of date Super Noodles and an entire Twix Easter Egg.

Things could always be worse.
   We could have Coronavirus.

* * *

- **What are you despairing about?**
- **What regrets do you hold?**
- **What wold you like to have done differently?**
- **How can you do something differently now?**

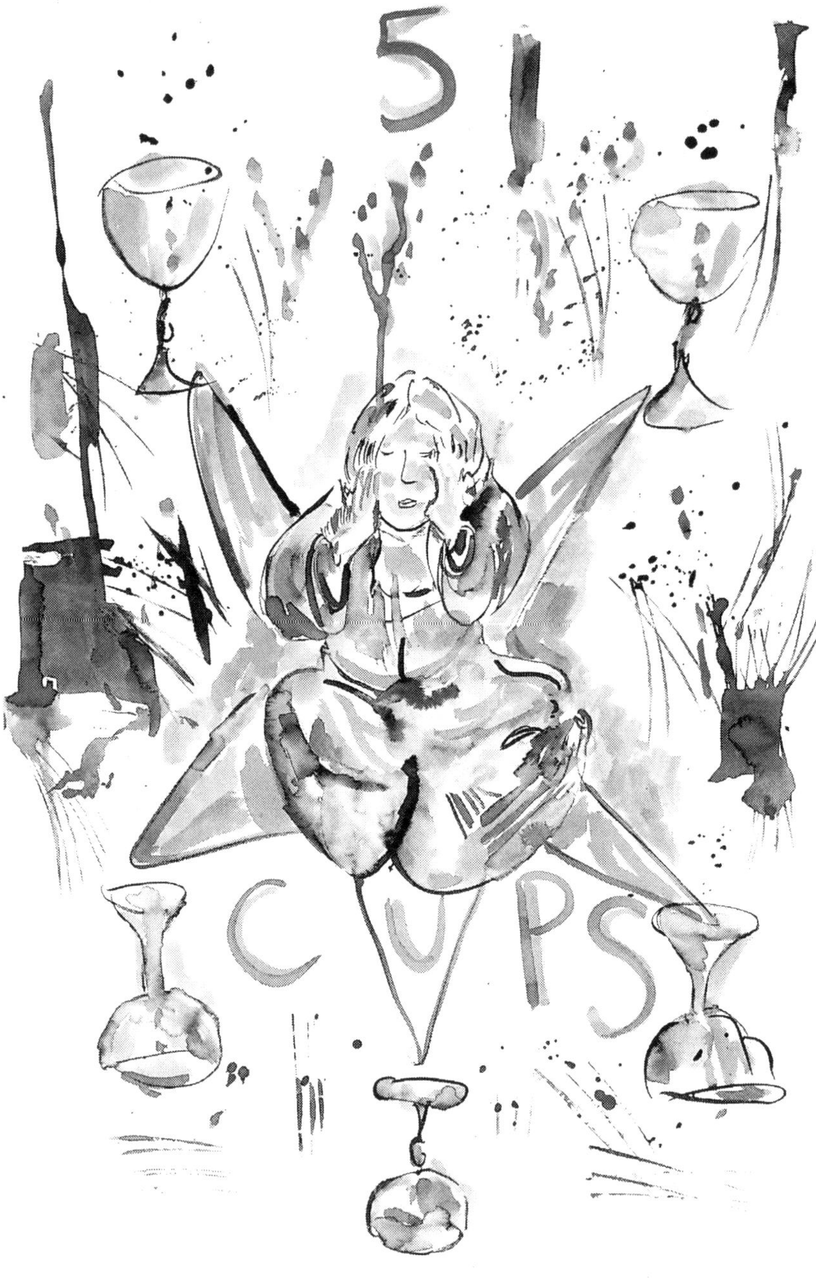
5
CUPS

42

6 of Cups

Plentifulness/Deficit

I must tell you that the supply of words on the world market is plentiful, but the demand is falling.

-Lech Walesa

In the deck I have this one looks quite rude. A naked woman with very large cups is stood in front of some gushing fountains.

Abundance and pleasure.

Live Laugh Love; Bumper stickers on her bumpers.

More is more and bigger is better.

Bulk buying of mantras and Goop products.

As I seek support to get this fucking thing finished, I join a group of budding self help writers.

Thousands of books on mindful this and tapping that and crystal healing nutri-shakes and Pilates for donut warriors.

I can balance five donuts on one hip.

We are over saturated. Over- mindful. If I see the phrase 'mental wellbeing seminar' or 'trauma summit webinar' in my inbox again, I will cry.

PowerPoints of brain diagrams just steal my life. They don't make me less depressed.

My mindful colouring looks like a felt-tip got killed.

I DO NOT want a 12- step plan to clear my clutter or meditate to frog chimes.

I am happy with my donuts and my misery.

I need no new friends, gadgets, underwear or Himalayan gongs.

I just want to be me.

Which is sometimes small and cynical with sagging boobs and a power point presentation about how much I hate power-point presentations.

***

- **How are you abundant and plentiful?**
- **Where do you feel depleted?**
- **Can you give away more?**
- **What offers can you say yes to?**
- **What can you say no to?**

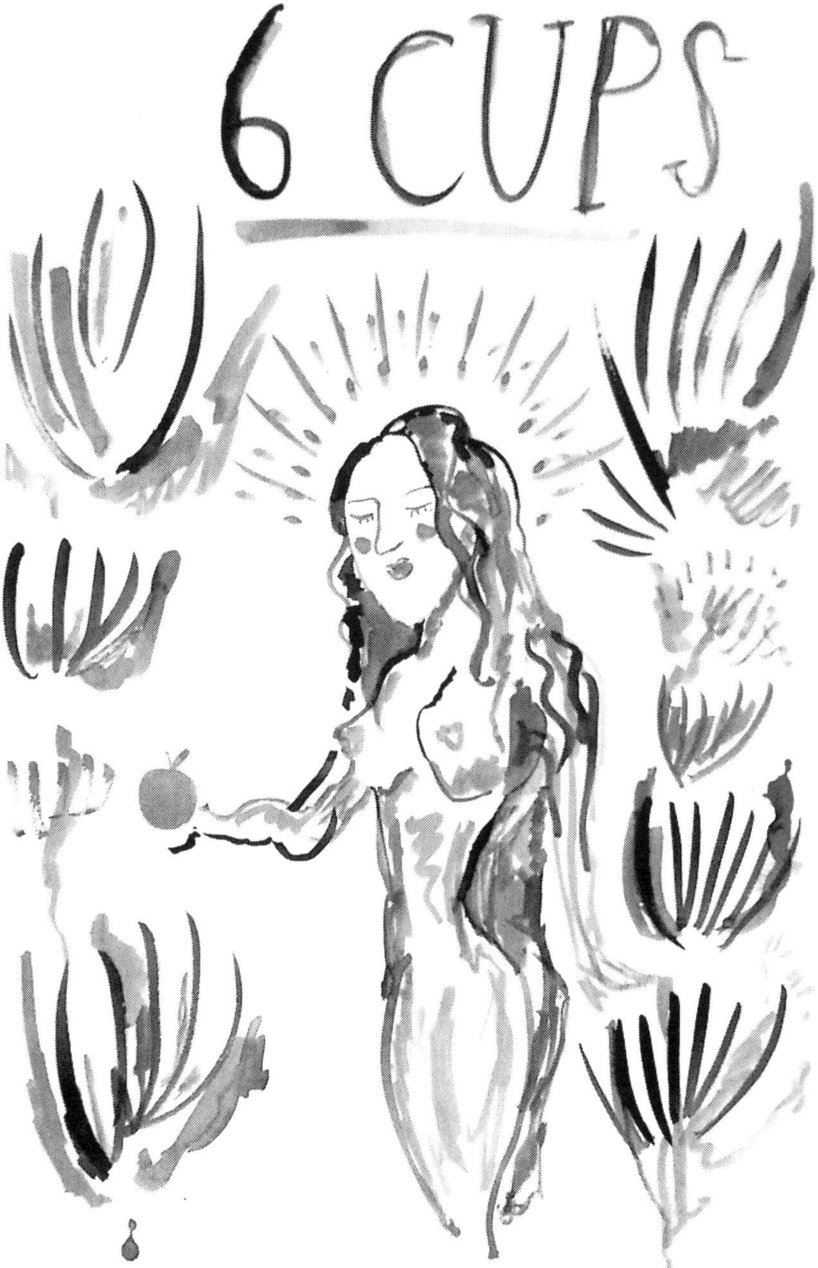
6 CUPS

43

7 of Cups

Imagination/Illusion

If we choose, we can live in a world of comforting illusion.

-Noam Chomsky

The cups in this card contain 7 treasures:

A head
   Some laurel leaves
   A snake
   A statue
   A castle
   Some jewels
   A baby dragon

Beneath these cups of treasure, floating in the arcade of the sky, is a rough sea not unlike Hastings, with traces of the big scary mummy sea dragon's tail. Flipping some poor knight, like a pancake, for dinner no doubt.

Her tail alone is nine mini castles wide.

Maybe she's got something to do with the severed head. A pancake topping?

This card reminds me of addictions, illusions, indulgences and ill afforded luxuries. Credit card spends and castles in the sky.
Illusions of grandeur.

Outbursts of ill advised rage. -Oops, did I press send on that email to my line manager?

Really this card is a bit of a bad dream. Like the Greek myths. Things rarely end well without bloodshed or fire.

I made a small paper puppet yesterday during the fairy tale workshop I was running. A princess called Burgundy who drinks too much wine at royal parties, as a way to be confident.

She has stigmata-like heart tattoos on her palms and a sash made of embroidered blue ribbon. Her mouth is turned down and sad. Her eyes pink glazed buttons.
Life in the castle with her many princess sisters doesn't work out well for her. She ends up making a fool of herself by drinking till she passes out most nights.

This was me in my 20's. It would be funny if it wasn't so sad.

I created her a little paper detox temple. I imagined her getting up at 5 to do morning payer. I also collaged her some powerful green powdery medicine to cleanse her system.

And gave her the gift of solitude and isolation by using pink gaffa tape around her tower. Away from the dragons, snakes and decapitations.

This is pretty much what I need right now. Time away from all the ways

I sabotage myself. Not with wine anymore but with so called friends who don't nourish me, work that's backbreaking and poorly paid, or food that makes me as fat as mummy dragon.

   I need a gaffa tape temple.

I have to find it in my body. I write this at 5.30am in an act of prayer.

* * *

- **What lies do you tell yourself?**
- **How do you self sabotage yourself?**
- **What gifts of kindness can you offer yourself?**
- **How can you be more kind to others?**
- **What does your body need?**

7 OF CUPS

175

44

8 of Cups

Longing/Implacability

Art is longing. You never arrive, but you keep going in the hope that you will.

-Anselm Kiefer

This card is a bit like the jump before you are pushed card. You know the sticky end is coming, so don't prolong it.

Get out of that relationship that you know will just implode anyway. Leave the job that can't offer any new opportunities for growth. Flee the crime scene before it's committed.

I find this card exceptionally hard. I cling onto my comfy, familiar, outdated modes for dear life. I never upgrade my phone or my wardrobe. I can't throw away the Christmas cards from three years ago.

It contains both the Sun and the Moon.

Its like that moment before dawn when the night cracks open.

8 OF CUPS

Be ready for the dawn.

Change is guaranteed. Uncertainty is certain and dark nights of the soul will always follow hay days.

Sign on the dotted line before the hand is forced.

Leave the abusive partner.
   Quit the drink.
   Move to that city.
   Take that class.
   Put in that boundary.
   Dust that mantelpiece.
   Phone that old friend.
   Ditch that whiney mate.
   Get out whiles the goings good and strike whilst the iron is hot.

Go hard or go home.

Don't put the future off.

Or cling to past nostalgia.

A new boat is coming.
   A new dawn is breaking.

As David Whyte, the poet says ' get ready to be ready'.

* * *

* * *

- What are you secretly longing for?
- What's your hearts desire?
- What are you hungry for?
- Make a desire map or a vision board collage.

8 OF CUPS

45

9 of Cups

Luxury/Overindulgence

In an age where overindulgence seems to be the norm, I can't help but look back and feel thankful that my parents chose to hold out on giving me everything that I wanted growing up.

-Dan Levy

The thing I overindulge most in is busyness.

Being a busy bee. This card contains many bees and their honeycomb. I am often busy trying to make my money for my honey.
  Working to avoid being.

Busy bee-ing to avoid doing the work I should be doing.

The sacred work of pure loving presence.

I joined a gratitude Facebook group. I kind of hate my entries, mainly because mine end up looking like a sentimental shopping list rather than an embodied experience.

    Gratitude can't be listed. Only felt. Like the first hug of the day. Or, god forbid, week. Gratitude is like a plant. It doesn't need just the water of polite recognition. It needs pure light.

In order to make the most of the light, gratitude needs to remember the dark times. The times when things weren't a given.

The times when water was scarce and so was company. The times when we struggled and fell on our knees and quit.
    I am grateful I am a survivor . In order to tell my story and help others trapped in the same story.

I am grateful I lost a home. So that the humble one I have now always seems like a palace.

I am grateful I terminated a pregnancy. So that I knew what it was like to make an impossible choice.

I am grateful I didn't drown the time I very nearly died. I had so much left to give.

I am grateful I had a zillion painful heartbreaks that led me to Triston and gave way for a zillion more.

I am grateful I gave up some of my addictive shit. It's given me so much more free space to get busy with.

Busyness is next. Busy giving it up.
    We need the busy equivalent of nicotine patches. Slow-the-fuck-down patches. Pop one on and meditate.
    Forget meditate. Just bee.

* * *

- What luxuries could you afford yourself this week/month?
- How can you give yourself luxury without spending money?
- How can you make more time for yourself?
- How does busyness get in the way of what you want to do?

9 OF CUPS

46

10 of Cups

Fulfilment/Delusion

In a position of utter desolation, when man cannot express himself in positive action, when his only achievement may consist in enduring his sufferings in the right way – an honourable way – in such a position man can, through loving contemplation of the image he carries of his beloved, achieve fulfilment.

–Viktor E. Frankl

A toast:

Ten time travellers in grey governess dresses toast an overflowing chalice

During lockdown I watched a version of Jane Eyre

All the theatres are steaming free shows

If I'm honest these have been my highlights

My portals into the imaginal

10 OF CUPS

This well dressed troupe in a horse and cart, clacking coconuts, references for a Mr Rochester

We are here to take care of the children Sir

Dolls houses with invisible attics where the help sleeps

Lace dresses from France
   Beribboned hair
   Not for the governess

Jane Eyre was the only classic I ever read
   Her grey eyes
   Like mine

Grace Poole in the attic is all of the never got overs
   Sealed with brown tape in cardboard boxes
   If I let them out they would flutter out like moths

The complex grief

Corners eaten away by mouse brown mice

The colour of my hair

I stared emptily at the dental section of the toiletries aisle today for what seemed like an eternity

Minty fresh, smokers choice, aloe-dent, baking soda, triple stripe, flossy picks, wire pokey things

Like the complex grief nothing is quite get out-able of the in-betweens

The dark dresses hold a multitude of grief stains in the folds

Smeared, lodged, wiped, deposited

He had talked about the girl that defecated on the floor

The Sun shone through the window

You walked into your room and never came out

No ribbons
   Mouse brown hair
   Grey starched dress
   Matching eyes

Toasting your disappearance

* * *

* * *

- **How are you deluding yourself?**
- **Who are you having a fantasy relationship with?**
- **Who or what fulfils you?**
- **What or who can you give a toast to?**
- **Do a ceremony for giving something up and taking something on**

10 OF CUPS

47

Knave of Cups

Intensity/Superficiality

I was a goth in my student days. I dyed my hair black, but it came out grey, with a blue scalp. Then I dyed it red and it came out fuchsia pink.

-Alice Roberts

She is Mystic Meg the psychic card.

I do believe that some hyper- sensitive people have a kind of sixth sense.

My mum who is a deeply sensitive empath hears songs that give her a weird thought about someone long forgotten and it will have turned out that they died at that moment.

Another relative who can't bare noise has sleep paralysis that brings visions of angels.

I've worked with autistic children who have a deep interest and respect for the concept of afterlife. They communicate with dead pets and whisper prayers through their oil pastel drawings of hamsters past.

At one time, those we now deem psychotic may have been the village shamans.

Dreaming on behalf of the community.

Like William Blake and his visions of angels and demons.

We all have a mad woman in the attic within us, bunny boiling. Or a mad man who's power crazy.

We have to keep it all in check.
   i.e. those fridge magnets that say 'Jesus is Coming... look busy'.

Busy or at least look like something passing as normal.
   None of us are normal. We are all mad here.

We just pretend not to be.
   The Knave of Cups delights in this.

She's like the goth girl in bus stops who wears pink fishnets, great big purple patent DMs, black leather tasselled jackets, embroidered with skate punk patches, a My Little Pony pink tshirt, green hair and a fluffy backpack with dinosaur spikes on.

She's playful, tough, soft, pierced, tattooed and dark at the same time.

I'd like to hope she may dress like that forever late into her cronehood. That wonderful poem 'start wearing purple' comes to mind.

There's an old woman with a hairy chin, stripy stockings and mini skirts who hangs out at Asda car park. If you get near her or look at her she accuses you of molesting her.

I wonder what she's been through.

Goth girl is great but she needs to find the light too.

Like glow worms in the dark….

Normal people.

* * *

- **Do you embrace your Sixth Sense?**
- **Do you think you are normal?**
- **What's your weirdest quirk?**
- **Do you embrace your darkness and your strangeness?**
- **Start wearing Purple**

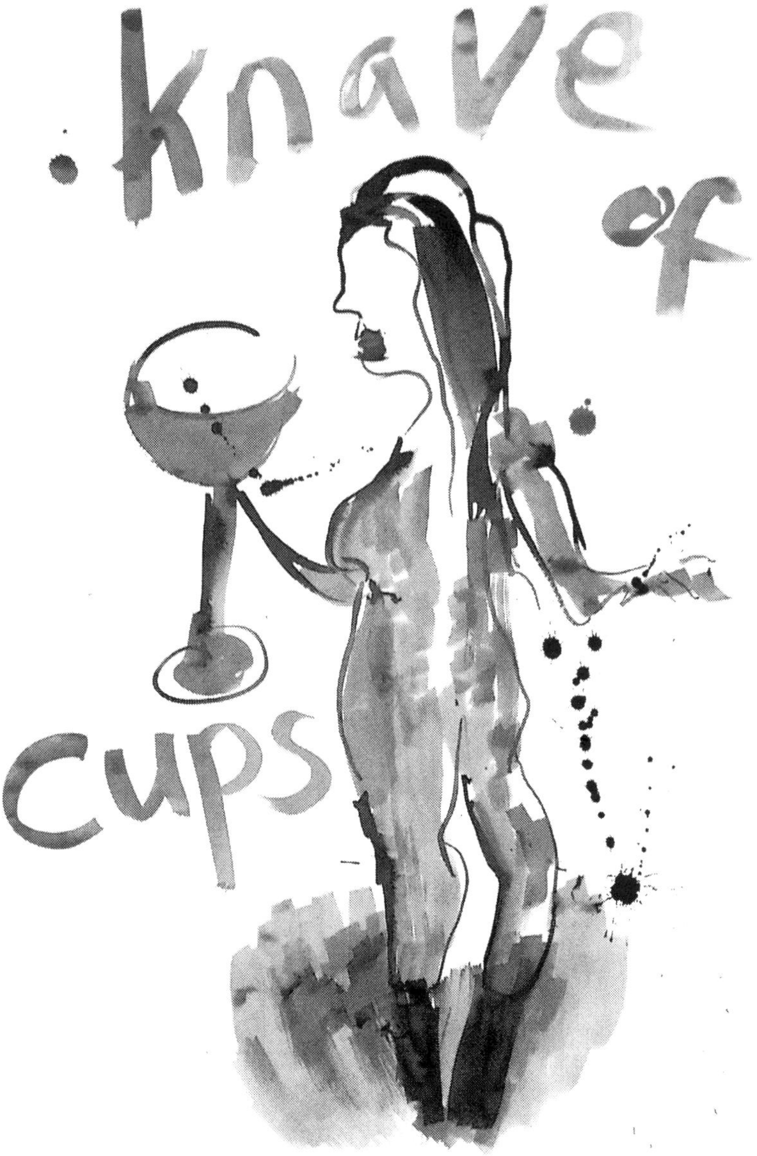
knave
of
cups

48

Knight of Cups

Zeal/Intolerance

Intolerance is evidence of impotence.

-Aleister Crowley

This card basically reminds me of those awful calendars with naked firemen holding hoses in just the right places.

Do you remember those Athena posters in the 80's with muscular men cradling premature babies in a sepia filter to highlight their abs?

I had one on my wall when I was 12, an act of me affirming to my parents that I was a) straight, despite snogging my best friend Michelle playing truth or dare at a sleepover and b) no longer interested in riding only My Little Ponies.

I am often affronted by women selling their bodies as a commodity, and sometimes I'm just as affronted when men do it (I wasn't affronted by much except homework when I was 12, hence the poor taste in wall adornment).

These days 12 year olds are so much cooler they probably have posters of kick arse girls Greta Thunberg, Emma Watson or Billy Eilish.

Call me unenlightened but the body is sacred and we too often are forced to value it in terms of poster- worthiness.

Athena may have closed down but Instagram opened up.

This Knight of Cups makes me think of a couple of men I have met at various conscious dance classes.

Despite their ability to sob during an Enya track and wear hemp sexily, some of them still look forward to the writhing transcendental tracks. Whereupon they may consciously rub against some fit yoga woman's toned thighs in the name of some ancient chakra balancing ritual.

I still can't trust Russell Brand even though I really like his 12 step recovery book. Mainly because of the fake ripped tshirts and Jesus beard/bead combo.

I have an innate distrust of kindness in men. I'm always wondering what the catch is. This comes after years of awful men in my life from an early age.
   When I hear my husband swearing at the computer in the room next door I still flinch like its my fault and say sorry.

I am working on being less distrusting of these knights, but its hard.

He has a superhero logo that contains three C's. Compassion, Care and Consideration. It all sounds quite chivalrous and, yes, zealous.
   But the shadow side is intolerance.

I know I am intolerant when a man can't be nice without me freaking out about what I need to give in return.

My editor sent me some really lovely writing feedback this week which made me feel happy on the inside and acknowledged.

Watch how I turn this into a new fear, I thought. Since then writing's felt harder.

My husband tolerates me very well. My constant trails of pants, art supplies, pens without lids and hair grips.

The way I balance the loo roll on top of the holder rather than change it. Or cook like someone who massively avoids cooking.

Not quite sure how he puts up with me sometimes. (And yes I'm not far off that 12 year old in terms of my ability to 'adult').

I'm so glad he does. He's taught me that men with the 3 C's do in fact actually exist and they don't need to hold baby chicks or wear leather to be beautiful.

I am slowly learning to change the loo roll and know that I am enough to deserve him.

I am also learning that I have cups of C's to offer too:

Calamity Creativity
And all the other best C words.

*　*　*

- **What broke your trust?**
- **Who do you trust?**
- **What do you tolerate?**
- **What will you no longer tolerate?**
- **Make a list of non negotiables**

KNIGHT OF CUPS

49

Queen of Cups

Empathy/Pity

It's hard to penetrate characters who are very cut off and lack empathy and to do it with sympathy. It's so easy to make a damaged character repugnant.

-Siri Hustvedt

This card somehow makes me laugh.

It reminds me of all the women with linen tent dresses, colourful embroidered scarves and 'ethnic' jewellery who I meet at therapy conventions.

Sometimes I am one.

After all, I love a jazzy scarf and some hand-fired clay beads.

I'm sure to become more of one in later years when I have more time or servants to iron linen.
  Empathy has its place in therapy.
  But so does a fight.

I fight to still wear a push up bra under my grey woollen shawls. Or swear in front of clients.

And not see addiction as separate from the collective experience. We are all fucked.

Yes even the women who go on cruises to Goa and shop at Waitrose and bake their own organic self importance.

The shadow side of this empathic elder woman is a character played by Emma Thompson in Noah Baumbach's film ' The Meyorwitz stories'. The escapades of a semi- bohemian, Jewish, dysfunctional family (my favourite film genre).

I'm sure I was a Jewish, New York talking therapist in a previous life. You know, the ones in all the films.

Anyway Thompson plays Dustin Hoffman's third wife Maureen. She wears the perfect tie-dye therapy outfits and has all the tissue boxes at the ready but is a total nutso alcoholic narcissist.

Her character is so spot on.

I remember this woman I used to work for in London, who shall remain nameless.

She used to do 'twinkly hands' to command a room and then send me emails of pure venom.

She was more interested in her amateur theatre productions of pantomimes at the Norwood playhouse than therapy. But refused to retire and make room for anyone. She still seemed to be remarkably into fake tanning, wearing more glitzy bangles than a gypsy harlot, and being chair of everything.

She would tell me at length how ill her husband Norman was and what an imposition this was to her luncheon dates.

She once hissed at me and nearly turned me to stone for daring to ask for travel expenses when I saved her arse by running a free workshop for her. One that she was no doubt being paid for whilst directing her village players version of the Wizard of Oz whilst I conducted a trauma CPD for social workers on a Saturday at the Croydon Holiday Inn.

She would make everyone perform a painful series of meet and greet activities at every workshop. Then the rest of it was mainly about her.

Empathy contains the word path. I think you probably need to have walked the path before you can truly empathise.

Otherwise it's just sympathy with more sterling silver accessories and Kleenex.

Twinkly hands and fun name games don't mean you've walked down the yellow brick road.

*Dorothy was not her real name

*　*　*

- **When is tea and sympathy needed?**
- **When is true empathy needed?**
- **Put yourself in the shoes of another but keep your socks on.**
- **When was the last time you moped in self-pity?**
- **Make a gratitude list**

THE WONKY WOMAN'S GUIDE TO TAROT

50

King of Cups

Composure/Rigidity

When your private life has been dragged into public space, you tend to attain a zen-like composure.

-Kalki Koechlin

This card always reminds me of the tale of the fisherman whose wife kept pressuring him to go for bigger and bigger wishes to the magic wish-giving fish.

They wanted for more and more until they came full circle and ended up back in their humble fisherman's hovel.

Back where I guess they somehow belonged.

I never got the impression that the fisherman was that bothered. He just felt very hen-pecked by his nagging wife and wanted for little more than a quiet life.

The King of Cups has a fish leaping from his cup but he has a steady unwavering quality to him.

Whether at sea in all weathers or commanding a vast banquet of fruits de mer.

Like King Neptune commanding the oceans with place settings and big beard wiping napkins.

I've been researching the late film maker and AIDS activist Derek Jarman and his gorgeously handsome partner the, also late, Keith Collins (who he nicknamed Hinney Beast). Keith cared for Derek in his little fisherman's cottage by the nuclear power plant at Dungeness.

After Derek died Keith apprenticed as a fisherman. Spending hours at sea and coming on land to tend to Derek's beautiful wild sea garden which he cared for painstakingly for many years after his beloved's death.

I love living in a fishing town. The leather-faced men with their nets and waders.

Communities who have fished for several generations.

The rickety black fishing huts that look akin to Baba Yaga's Human Steak house.

The pirate flags flying on old cracked boats and broken crabs legs scattered amongst the stones.

Derek would be a King of Cups. Commanding the actors, who were often his friends, in his experimental films.

Like Jesus with 12 disciples he broke the bread and uncorked the wine.

All at his table were fed from his creative energy he didn't need a wish fish or a wife.

Just Keith and his kindness.

* * *

- **What life have you composed?**
- **Who are the 12 disciples at your table? These could be icons, artists, film makers, musicians, speakers; both dead or alive.**
- **What is stuck?**
- **Who could help you?**
- **Compose some letters. Send the ones you want to, burn the rest.**

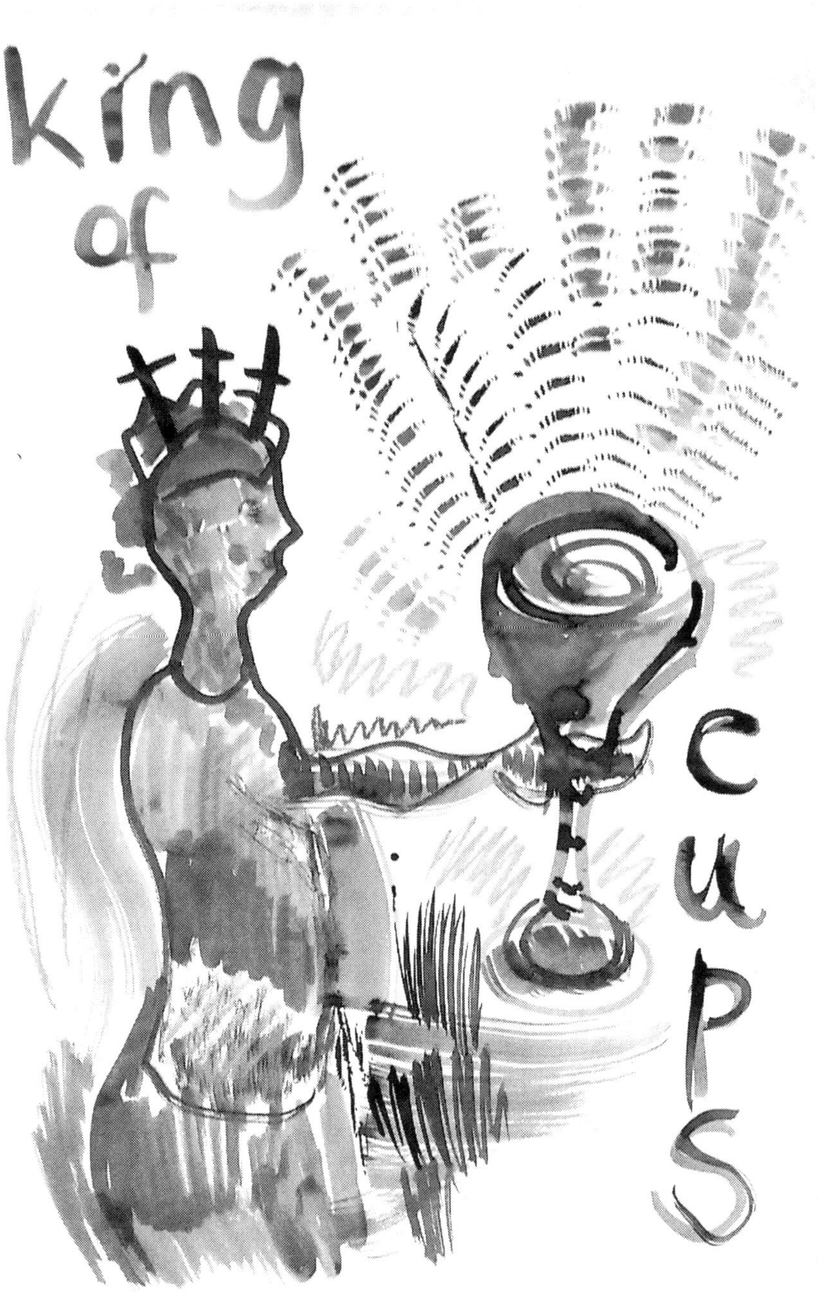
king of
cups

51

Ace of Swords

Objectivity/Slyness

Objective
adjective

1. *Not influenced by personal feelings or opinions in considering and representing facts.*
2. *Not dependent on the mind for existence; actual.*

I tend to find it hard to be objective about anything. I live firmly in the subjective realms. I chose a career path based on feelings and hunches as opposed to goals and practicality. Maybe my goal was in fact to be closer to feelings than facts.

Art is my world and it is largely subjective. Tears channelled through brushstrokes and photographs that capture a precious snapshot of the subject's inner world.

I guess artists like Pier Mondrian, Anthony Caro and Bridget Riley are considered to be more objective artists, but this is not entirely true. Yes they use sparse grids, lines, planes and geometrical forms but even this engenders soul echoes of life's uniformity, patterns, rigidity and space.

In my mind objectivity is linear and subjectivity is squiggly and wiggly. Life is rarely the former and often the later.

My husband, on the other side of the bed lives in the objective isles. His bedside table (if we had them) would have perhaps a watch and a shopping list on, mine a pack of tarot cards and a shrine to chaos. He's a scientist and his world is based around measuring, fixing, analysing and recording.

Together it's a wonder how we function. But in many ways we balance one another out like Jack Sprat and his plump wife.

I guess where slyness comes into all this is that, slyly, objectivity creeps into my life.

I have realised over the years that routine is the saviour that stops me going mad. Rituals are manageable practical measures I take to stay grounded.

Night and day are important, the four seasons, alarm clocks and set meal times. These dependable rhythms hold me though all of my subjective wobbles.

For years I resisted the linear path of long term commitment but coming home to the same warm embrace of my husband's body day after day is really all that home now means.

Slyly, I have also injected subjectivity into my husband's world. We are spontaneous with our foreign film choices, I mess up his matching sock regime and hopefully I have beguiled him with my feminine mystery which, quite frankly, is more erratic than subjective.

This card containing both a wreath of holly and a blade is a homage to all things sharp. Sharp was in fact my birth surname which I changed for many reasons. Maybe beneath my womanly softness I still know how to wield a mutherf*cker of a blade.

In order to sharpen the sword I must obey the order of all things, stick to my 9 to 5 sometimes, instead of slacking it off to buy colourful leggings from Taiwan on the internet.

I must find routine in the linear as well as the circular so that A to B doesn't always bite me on the arse.

Clear routes and objective landmarks on the way so that I can find life's red berries beneath the spiked leaves and remember the path to return.

Love, after all, is like objectivity, in that it does not depend on the mind for existence. It depends on the heart.

* * *

- **Make art with only straight clean lines thinking about goals**
- **Make art with only wiggly lines thinking about feelings**
- **Mix them together**

Ace of Swords

52

2 of Swords

Truce/Impasse

What has happened in the years since the Second World War is not a temporary truce. It is not simply a ceasefire. Instead of battling with weapons and armaments, people battle only with arguments and ideas.

-Gordon Brown

This card is about re-centring. Do not cross.
   The time out card.

A woman sits blindfolded holding two swords defensively across her face and body. I had a whole week off writing this week.
   Each night I came home from long days of working and teaching.

Ate dinner and promptly passed out with exhaustion before doing it all over again.

Didn't do my morning exercise, meditation practice, wash my hair or answer many e-mails this week.

Simply did the bare minimum to survive the week of punishing hours and cold February days. Not writing made me sad. It's the last thing I have time for and the one thing I really want to do. I bottled it up and saved it for today.

A nine hour coach trip to Yorkshire to see my poorly father.

Much time to write myself back to life, as my feet get pins and needles on the National Express 426 to South Shields.

I almost regret giving my neck pillow to a homeless man lying with his head on the concrete pavement.

But no. He needed it more than me.

Sometimes I go through my days like the blindfolded woman. Two swords at my chest telling everyone to keep a wide birth. I'm on my period you fuckwits. Keep away!

At the heart of the fuck off swords is the vulnerability of the woman who cannot see. She cannot see how to get through the day or week, let alone month.
  She cannot see how loved and protected she is. She cannot see beyond the endless to do list.
  She must re centre in her own body. Sew her head back on her own neck. Sit in a dark room and completely shut down. She needs to go within.
  All that surrounds her is perceived as potential threat. Even those that come in peace.

In these times everything genuinely is a threat because the outer life constantly calls her away from her life preserving inner world.

She needs to stop and rest in a defended sanctuary of her own making. Even if it is a 7 hour bus schlep to York via Doncaster.

At least they have chargers on board.

* * *

* * *

- **What do you need to call time on?**
- **Who can you make a truce with?**
- **What demon in yourself can you lay to rest?**
- **How can you go easier on yourself today?**

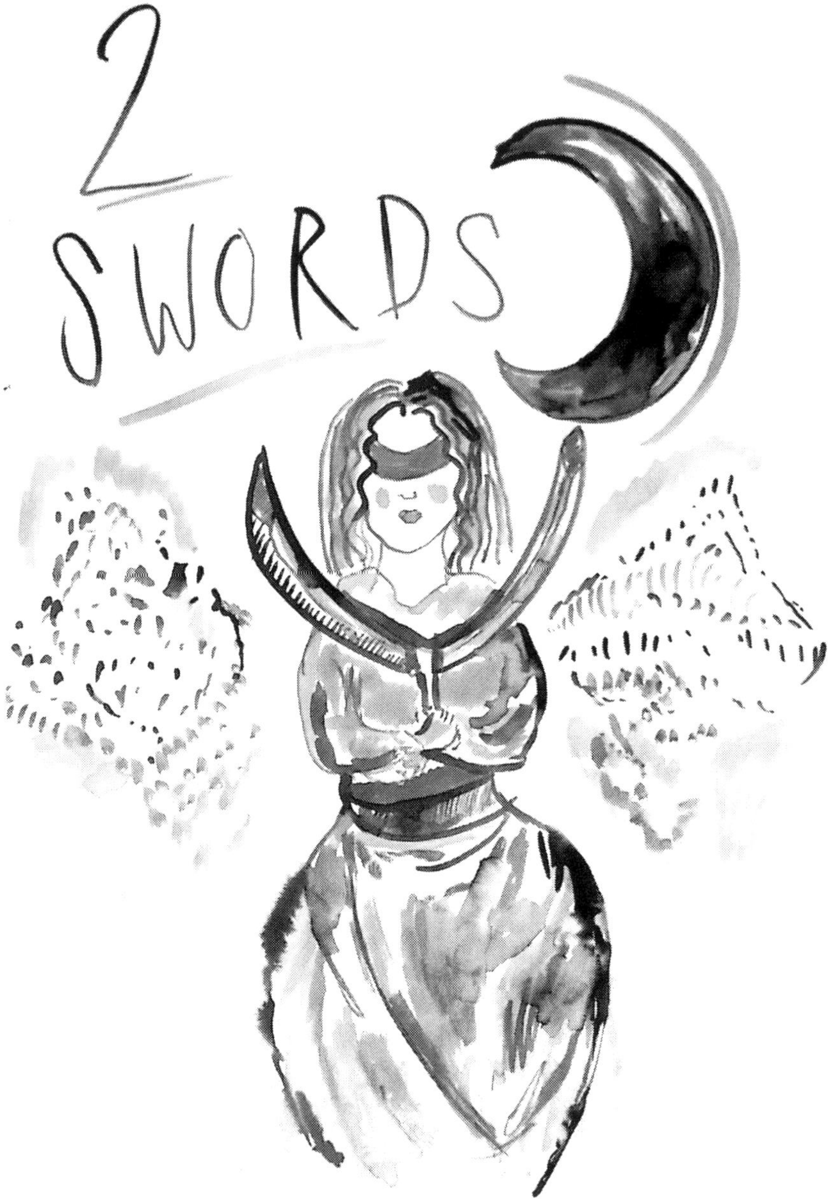
2
SWORDS

53

3 of Swords

Clarity/Heartbreak

I have this sense of independent heartbreak, of annulling romances before they get their feet off the ground.

-Timothee Chalamet

Two years ago my husbands friend Tom lost the love of his life to cancer. Heartbreak has been etched into his life.

My husband and him, jog together on the seafront one morning a week. A way for Tom to move through the wall of heartbreak he feels every single day.

It haunts his days and nights.

He would do anything to turn back time; it's Valentines day next week and he's dreading it.

He dreads birthdays, Christmas and anniversaries containing any memories of their beauty filled time together.

They were together 15 years.
   I didn't get to know Tom till after his partner Naomi died.

My husband who knew him from the gym saw him on the beach sobbing one time.

We asked him in a text if he was OK; we knew he wasn't.
   We invited him for lunch and he showed us photos of them both on his phone.

Through it all he looks after plants as a gardener.
   He is so kind and tender towards each living shrub and emerging bloom.
   He knows that life is precious.
   Tom is precious to us.
   He reminds us that heartbreak can be lived day to day and survived.

He teaches us to be grateful. To have faith that love goes beyond even the deepest hurt. He teaches us that loss can't be buried.
   Only acknowledged and honoured day after day.

Him and my husband do squats, lunges, press ups and step ups together. They swear at the personal trainer under their breath and go for a pint after.
   He wipes a surreptitious tear when certain songs come on the radio.

His heartbreak is worth honouring.

* * *

- **Who or what broke your heart?**

- **Make a playlist of heartbreak songs**
- **What a tear jerking movie**
- **Cry into some wine or jog?**

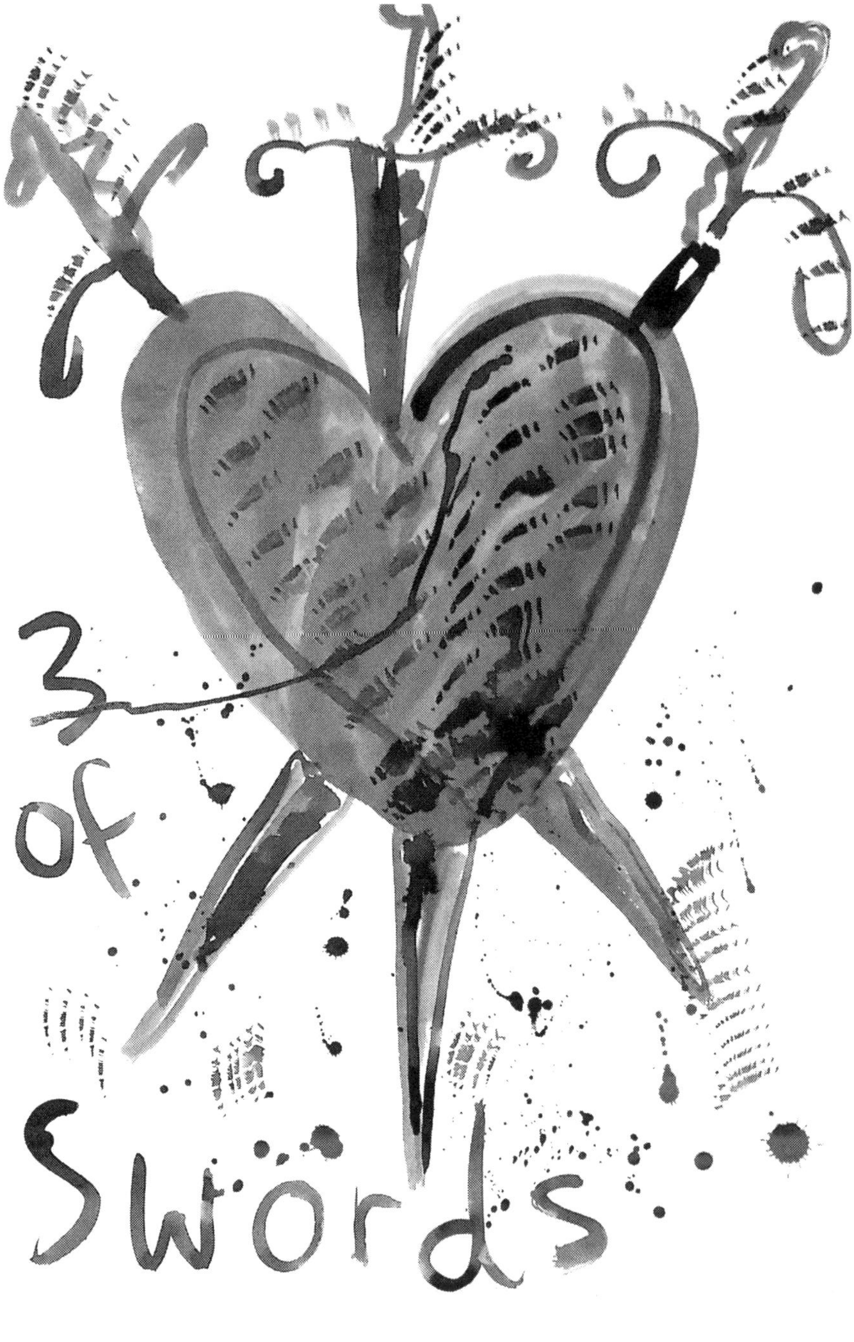
3 of Swords

54

4 of Swords

Contemplation/Procrastination.

Procrastination gives you time to consider divergent ideas, to think in nonlinear ways, to make unexpected leaps.

-Adam Grant

I will get round to writing about this at some point, I thought.

After I contemplate cleaning my fridge.
　The Christmas cheese still lurks at the back.

At New Year I normally do a spell of meditation. Not this year.
　'I'm stayin' busy.'

Busy doing fuck all. Not even cleaning the fridge.

My phone has become a procrastination machine.
　Contemplation has simply morphed into periods of kettle boiling anxiety. Being in stillness and silence feels impossible.

Background noise fills my life.

The fridge hums. The washing machine rattles. The oven buzzes. The heater gurns.

A kid in my youth group drew broken kitchen appliances today in a dark and dusty basement. I asked him if there was anything in his fridge.

'No it's off because it doesn't work' he grinned.
   I imagined opening the door. The stale vacuum of leaden air leaking out.

This kid has a dark basement situation going on for sure but at least he can draw it in HB pencil and see the funny side.

I thought about my unacknowledged basement fridge. The emotions I have trapped in a vacuum. I'd need charcoal or at least black oil pastel on parcel paper to describe it.

The places where nothing is kept fresh.

Rotten places. I guess these are what I avoid by not being still. In being still and attendant I have to see the unattended parts. The left overs. The strays. The ash trays. The fly-tip of my thoughts.
   The kid also drew a sewer full of rat eggs. 'Rats don't lay eggs' another kid piped. He just shrugged it off. 'They do in my head' he said.
   Procrastination. Contemplation.

Fridges and rats eggs.

* * *

- **What are you putting off?**

- What are you thinking about doing but not yet doing?
- What's inside your basement fridge?
- How can you approach what you are avoiding in a creative non linear way?

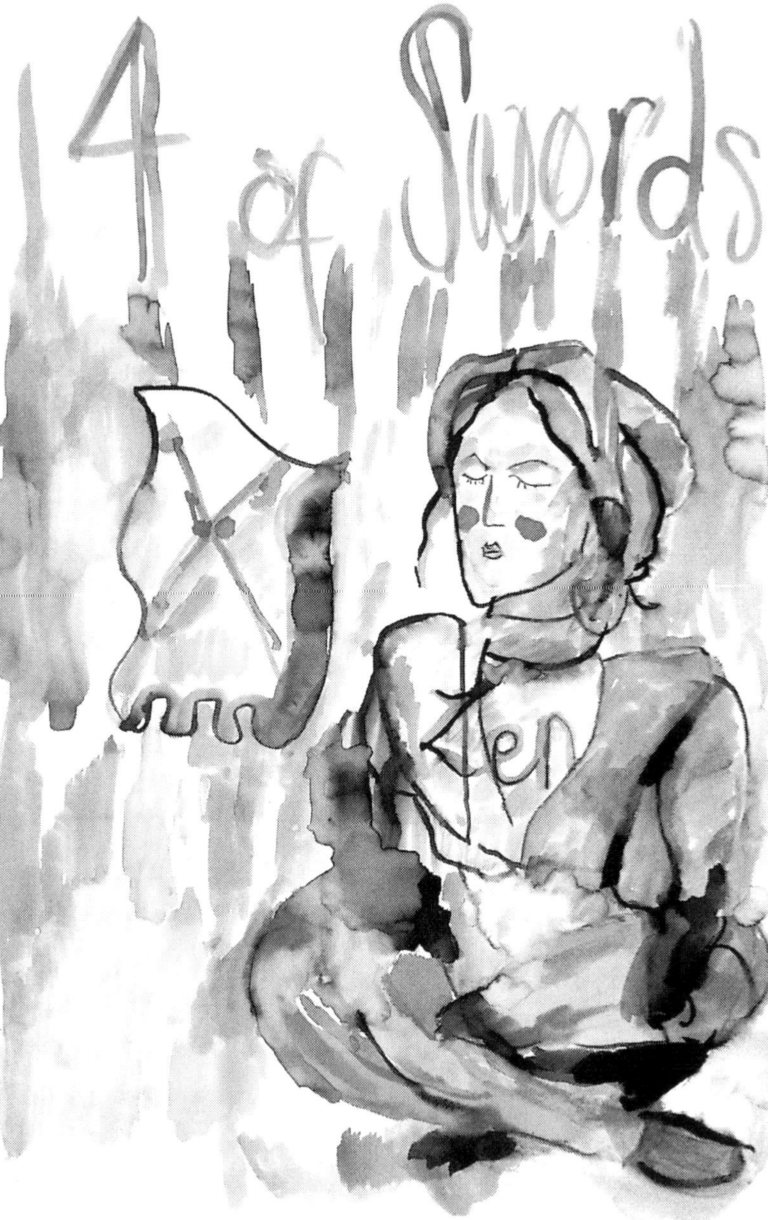
4 of Swords
Zen

55

5 of Swords

Individuality/Irrationality

I believe in individuality, that everybody is special, and it's up to them to find that quality and let it live.

-Grace Jones

Before we get into the two I's here, my first reaction is really to the powerful and emotive image on this card.

A vulnerable androgynous figure stands in the centre, wearing a mustard yellow tunic. Hands over their ears. Their posture looks fearful and hunched with unsteady footing. Surrounding them are 5 swords pointed at them with 5 people wearing green tunics turning their backs.

Really this image says so much.

It says more than just individuality and irrationality. Which to me are quite slippery concepts. Individual is as difficult to define as normal.

Immediately I think of the playground politics of the world. The bullies who have the power and the individuals whose uniqueness is held against them.

It makes me think of those with neurodiverse profiles who don't fit with the mainstream. Round pegs in square holes. The kids who get bullied or ignored because they are outsiders or love a knitted mustard tunic.

What's worse than having five swords pointed at you? Having 5 people's backs to you. The worst way to torture a person is to make them feel invisible or unheard.
   I work with many such children.

These children do possess invisibility cloaks and often that is just one superpower in their arsenal of survival hacks.

In the story of the 12 dancing princesses a wounded soldier (classic veteran with PTSD archetype) uses his invisibility cloak for good and follows the princesses stealthily to the underworld.

They underestimate him and write him off as a simpleton and yet he exposes them in the end and uncovers the truth. They didn't see it coming.

Being invisible restores sight to others. *Eventually.*

You used to be a right weirdo if you were a vegan (my mother still can't pronounce it — she says 'veygan' like its still only for vague, pale people).

Now everyone's at it with their trendy jackfruit nuggets and oat milk.

Tattoos and piercings used to signify a kind of rebellious counter culture and now even the bankers and estate agents have full sleeves and an undercut.

We should perhaps all recognise our own unique weirdness and make efforts to celebrate it.

Reserve one afternoon walk around town per week to simply observe as an outsider.

Be the aliens. I guess that's why holidays are so refreshing. We see other cultures and realise how different people, places and climates are.

We recognise difference as actually just richness and diversity.

Like the bullies in this card we turn our backs many times a day. Whether its walking past the homeless guy outside Co-Op, without eye contact or ignoring the stirring symptoms that we know could lead to disaster.

In order not to turn our backs on love we may indeed have to witness real suffering which we can't then 'un-see'. At least in doing this we are acknowledging our own privilege, potency and potentiality.

Maybe we can even flip the sword to face the other way. No longer cornering the unfashionable and meek (who shall inherit the earth BTW) but facing the outer world.

Cutting out that which comes from outside influence so that the inside landscape of compassion and understanding takes the lead. Our individuality and inner life that goes beyond trends, fashions and being cool. Supporting those without privilege who have a different way of experiencing the cultural bias of the world.

* * *

- **What are your unique gifts?**
- **Who's been a bully in your life?**
- **What suffering in the world are you able to acknowledge?**
- **How can we make the world a better place with our special gifts?**

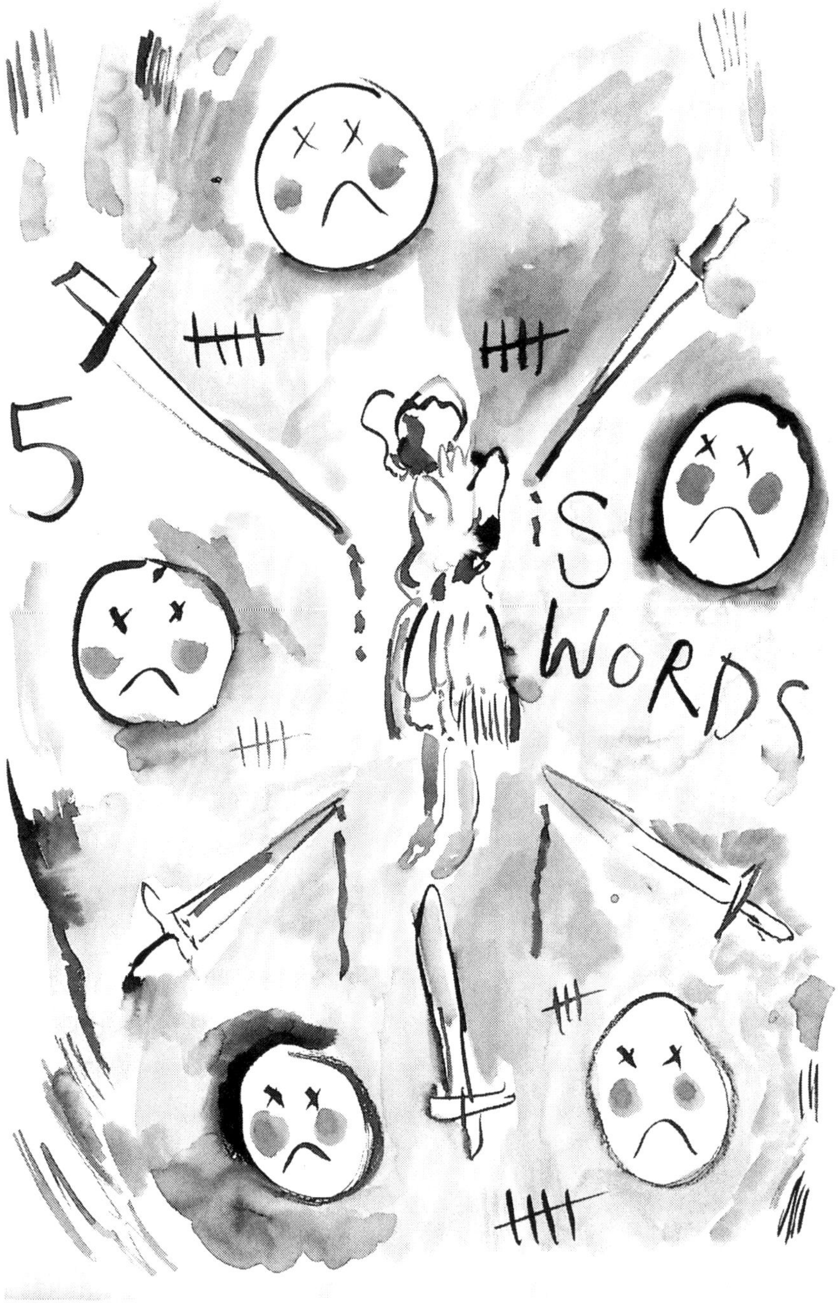
5
S
WORDS

56

6 of Swords

Perspective/Victimisation

That migrant families might be menaced or threatened in any way, shape or form when they arrive at our border – often times after an unimaginably arduous journey – is completely unacceptable.

-Michelle Lujan Grisham

Finding safe ground
   We will sail all night

Till we see a glimpse of God on the shore.

In Hastings recently a group of nudists on the beach helped rescue a group of migrant refugees.

Sometimes we have to really take a risk to find safety

Cross waters

Be with the unknown

Enter into a new world with different languages and customs.
   We have to lose everything

The oars row. Our arms ache

Our hearts ache for new land

For earth and bed and belonging

For respite from hunger and thirst and sickness

For a new kind of god
   One who doesn't punish or scorn

A culture where **other is mother**

Where the surf brings blank pages to lives

New starts

Safety
   Shelter
   Peace

You can land in the net, not slip through it

* * *

Patchwork pieces

6 OF SWORDS

You're at Dad's next weekend
Not sure when Mum's coming home
You'll be lucky to get kindness in the form of weak blackcurrant squash
And a custard cream
From well-meaning imposters
But you patchwork that heart of yours anyway
Your faith in this disappointing world is immense
You find colour where there is none
You find magic where adults argue
And fight custody battles
Your mothers marrying men just to flee your unsafe country
You have a pouch of precious things
Rainbows and poems
And songs
Your motherland is still sacred within you
The unstitched parts
Stored up tricks for rainy days
Puddles of pure love and forgiveness
Reminding your grown-ups of their forgotten resources
They would do anything to see you move beyond their own hurt

* * *

- Where is your shelter?
- Who is your safe harbour?
- What practice is your refuge? Art? Writing? Mediation?
- What needs rescuing in your life?
- Whose critical voices do you need to drown out?
- How can you welcome the exiled parts of yourself you don't like?

Six of Swords

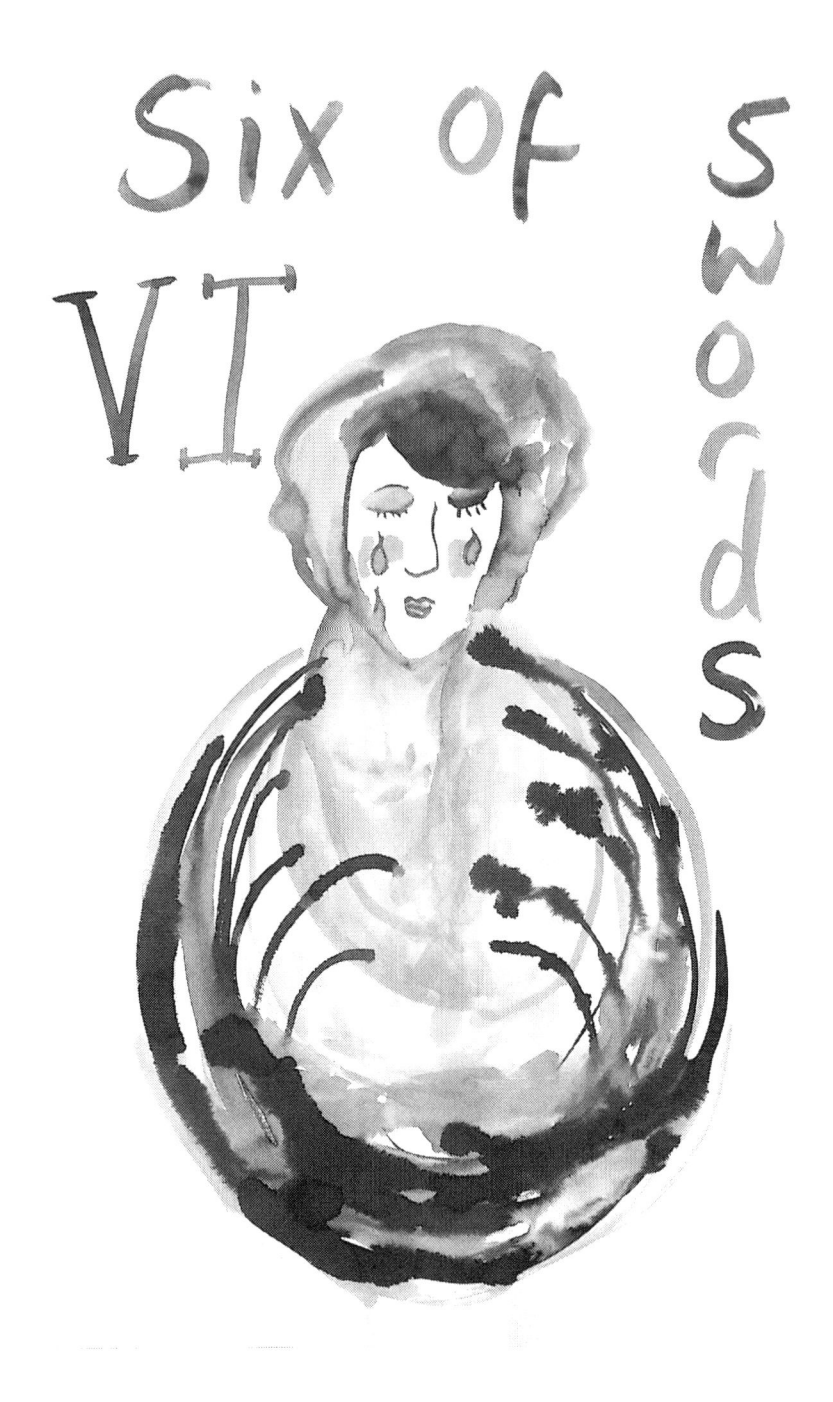

VI

57

7 of Swords

Justification/Presumption

We're all just animals. That's all we are, and everything else is just an elaborate justification of our instincts. That's where music comes from. And romantic poetry. And bad novels.

-Elvis Costello

This card is a bit dodgy.
    The guy's just sneaked an extra tin of beans through the self service checkout.

It's the card of those who are forced to justify their actions perhaps through the work that they do.

Thieves and pickpockets, or just those like me who steal the mini shower gels that smell of fake sea breeze from budget hotels.

Those who have presumed they could coast through life with minimal participation. (Always).

It makes me think of the times in my youth where I bunked trains and lessons. Now I bunk yearly appraisals and peer-review meetings.

It makes me think of the scary girl I allowed to steal my lunch money for years without telling anyone.

The woman who highjacked my teaching skills for her financial benefit.

My university tutors who photocopied crap handouts and spent lecturing time drinking 2 for 1 shots on student night.

Exes who choose to be bored and miserable rather than be of service in this world because they are true *artists* and no one gets them.

I have given my services away for minimum wage all my life. I have had dozens of crap jobs in retail.
   But I've always worked and been of service in some way.

I have mopped floors, poured pints, told women they look nice in hideous polyester gowns, sold ink cartridges, packs of menthol Superkings and large bottles of vodka to old women in remote villages where the One Stop is the nearest and last stop for them.

I have wiped the bums of kids I don't like and helped 4 year olds blow their noses when they aren't my children.

I have waited tables with plates of greasy fish and chips and emptied full ash trays in nicotine stained yellow ceilinged rooms before the smoking ban.

I have been spat at by kids at work. And sometimes sworn at; once I was even given a frog in a Tupperware lunchbox as a gift.

I've told people not to touch paintings in galleries and stolen paperclips and elastic bands from the stationary cupboard.

I was a pet sitter for aggressive geese, who once chased me round the neighbours' garden.
   I babysat kids, staying up late playing Mario Kart with them.

I presume nothing is a given and that my spending is usually hard won or justified.

Service is not about having a job that you absolutely love but the willingness to get up and do it even if you don't.

There are no shortcuts only lessons.

* * *

- **What have you begged, stolen, borrowed or blagged??**
- **Make an inventory**
- **What are you trying to justify getting away with?**
- **How can you be charitable?**

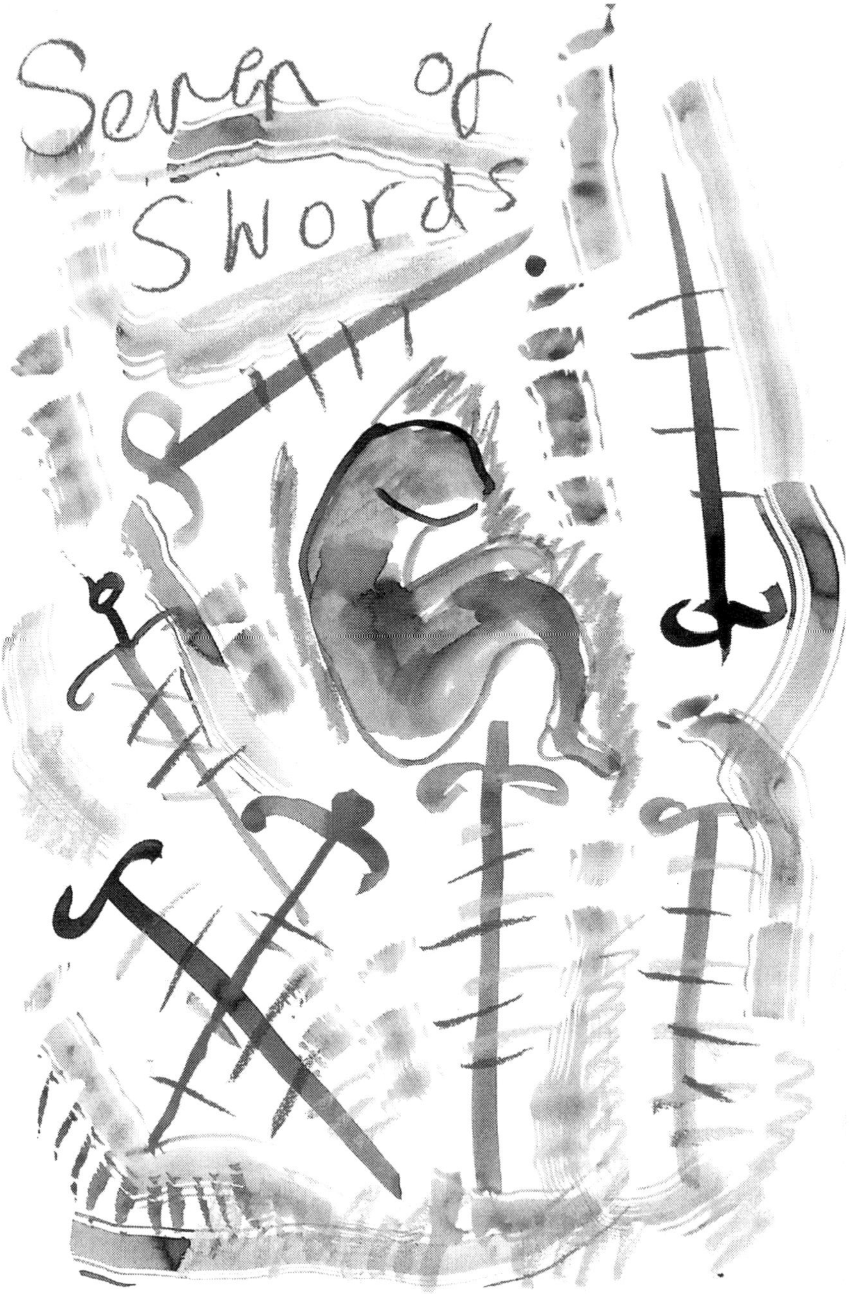
Seven of Swords

58

8 of Swords

Limits/Restrictions

The best restriction I learned was getting into the habit of doing something, even if I didn't feel like it, instead of running away from it. Sometimes good work needs to be earned, and when you can overcome yourself, the muse notices and celebrates.

-Damien Rice

Here she is bound

Unable to see
The ladder of opportunity lays before her

Creeping up it with only trust and the ground falling away

In order to climb she must simply trust

Hold on

Put one foot above the other

A step closer to the gods
But the empty feeling inside remains
I try reaching out through messages, texts, group chats and likes
But the loneliness doesn't end
Just me
My lonely heart
Missing who I have been
Longing for what I want to be
Stuck between places
Unable to move or switch or act
Just me
On this sofa
Just me
In this bath
When getting dressed
And eating feels like work
All activity is a distraction
From inactivity
Faith is scattered
Heart is splintered
Mind is spent
I can only call on love and ask that
love simply hold me
In all of my mess and inertia
In all of my unravelling
In my sadness
In my grief
The down days are when I need love most
And it can feel the hardest to reach
I must simply fall
And trust that the only way is up

* * *

- **What risks are you taking?**
- **What mystery are you making room for in your life?**
- **What are you trying too hard to control?**
- **What's the next baby step you need to take?**
- **Just get through today.**

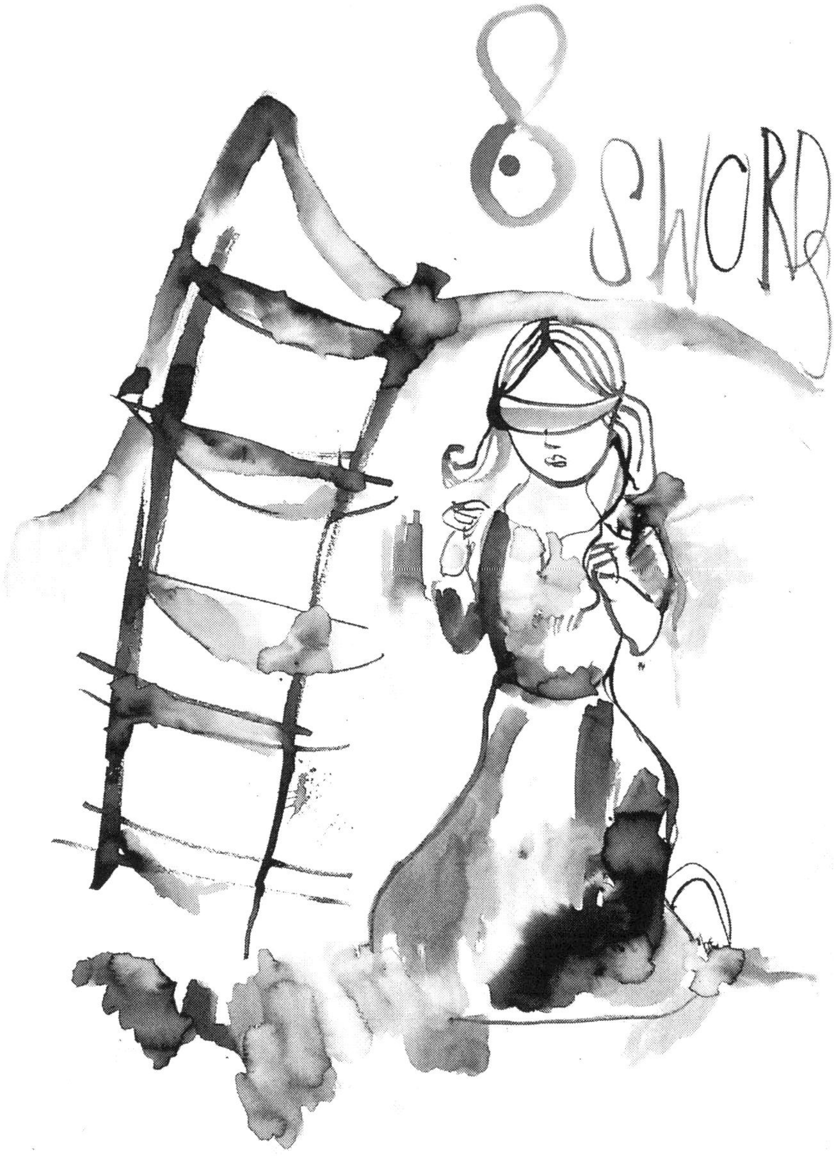
8
SWORDS

59

9 of Swords

Insight/Worry

Let me tell you something about full moons: kids don't care about full moons. They'll play in a full moon, no worries at all. They only get scared of magic or werewolves from stupid adults and their stupid adult stories.

-Neil deGrasse Tyson

Oh, the worry card!
   Had to pull it at some point.

Day three of illness in bed. Perfect day to go into the pits of anxiety and despair.

Was booked on a nourishing dance workshop tomorrow which I have cancelled as I don't want to cough over everyone.

My goal tomorrow is clean up the heap of used tissues under my bed and change the lurgee'd sheets. I also need to wash my matted hair and eat something other than soup.

I'm not a patient patient. I've had to cancel about 9 things in 3 days. Sat through 1 film, 2 documentaries, and about 11 YouTube videos today.

Britain also left the European Union, as if that wasn't trauma enough.

Left a crying voice message to my friend Melanie. Telling her I was glad she was my friend. Managed half a bowl of soup.

Two more WhatsApps to a friend who is not replying.

Anxiety of not being or doing enough coursing through my veins.

On the plus side, I found a great YouTube channel today and it made me feel alive.

Videos about all sorts of wonderful things creativity, dating, heartbreak, treasure, lost voices, found voices and risk.

I also watched my Course in Miracles monthly webinar.

My teachers were banging on about the past being over, the willingness to forgive being present and the future placed in the hands of the higher self.

If I follow those three basic things, anxiety gets a lot easier to manage and insight hooks in. After all, if the divine in me has got it, I'm good; I just need to forgive myself a little more.

For example my higher self guided me today to wear my white fluffy fleece that makes me feel like I live in Narnia.

A higher power guided me to watch a documentary about a sign language speaking chimp called Nim. What touched me most about Nim the chimp was that he brought so many people into their destiny.

Everyone who cared for Nim became extremely important in Nim's life story.
    It was touching watching grown men and women sobbing at the memories of caring for him. He recognised them all immediately in old footage of reunions.

Made me think of all the kids who I've been impacted by and had an impact on. These threads can feel invisible yet they never leave us.

Like Nim Chimpsky demonstrated, love is always recognizable.

My higher power made me watch a weird and wonderful documentary about the 50's film star Jayne Mansfield who was killed horrible in a car crash.

Life is full of car crashes and this card reminds us why we worry about getting into cars and driving full beam towards our destiny.

I spent my whole childhood stepping between cracks, not saying *yes* to anything and hiding in the shadows of others.
    I come from a long line of worriers.

Not warriors.
    Worriers.

Did I turn the stove off?
    Am I an alien?
    Is this normal? Am I too normal?
    When can I get off? Is my hair shit?
    Does he/she really like me?
    Why the fuck isn't my natural deodorant fucking working? What if I die?
    Oh shit I'm going to.

I love Susan Jeffers' book *Feel The Fear and Do It Anyway*.

It was a revelation to me when I realized even brave people still get scared, have doubts and crawl away from the world in Narnia fleeces sometimes.

Chimp documentary days happen to the best of us. We are all car crashes sometimes.

Repeat:

Tomorrow I will clean the tissues up.

***

- **What keeps you awake at night?**
- **Make a worry box to give your worries to post them then go and have a relaxing worry free bath with your favourite oils/rose petals/Epsom salts in.**
- **Make a worry doll.**
- **Are there any insights to be gained behind the fear?**
- **If you move through the fear what awaits you the other side?**

9 of swords

60

10 of Swords

Detachment/Ruin

If I take death into my life, acknowledge it, and face it squarely, I will free myself from the anxiety of death and the pettiness of life – and only then will I be free to become myself.

-Martin Heidegger

I think of this as the self injury card.

Fresh blood on the knives
   We are the sacrifice

Coming at us from all sides

We feel overwhelmed.

Why do we so often self harm and self sabotage?

Because it helps us cope

10 OF SWORDS

Takes us away from life's complex tapestry
   of chronic anxiety. Reminding us we are here and now. Flesh and blood.
We are alive.

We are not dead like the consumerist ghost towns we live in.

We are tribal. Marked by suffering, ritual and landmarks of the soul.

The landscape of the body is probed with holes.

Our spirits need places to blood let and allow for release.

It can simply be with red ink, wine, menstruation, acupuncture or tattoos;

Maybe poetry written by a broken heart.

Limbs that seek praise.
   Tributaries of the body.
   Where Red meets Blue and Blood meets Ocean.

Belonging to our bodies is hard.

Belonging to our lives is hard.

Belonging to our art saves us.

Sharpen the sword of the pencil or the nib of the fountain pen that writes
and draws and speaks the true names of all we are.

Beneath the body.

               * * *

- What are you feeling detached from?
- Can you feel your feet on the ground? Your lungs breathing? Your heart beating?
- How can you connect with your aliveness
- Connect with the present moment where heartbeat meets breath

10 OF SWORDS

61

Knave of Swords

Practice/Pretence

For Sabina, living in truth, lying neither to ourselves nor to others, was possible only away from the public: the moment someone keeps an eye on what we do, we involuntarily make allowances for that eye, and nothing we do is truthful. Having a public, keeping a public in mind, means living in lies.

-M. Kundera

This card makes me think of the character of Sabina in Milan Kundera's book *The Unbearable Lightness of Being*.

In a deliciously seductive chapter she strips totally naked for her lover Tomas, wearing only a bowler hat.

Her character, despite her bold eroticism, is actually quite wounded. Her sexuality and freedom is her only salve.

She spends her life avoiding what she feels to be the kitsch pursuits of marriage, motherhood and commitment, and her life becomes a series of wild betrayals and creatively executed affairs.

She believes that beauty is only ever beautiful if it's overlooked. Nothing mainstream contains this seed.

I love this idea. I also am deeply in love with her character. I would love to be her.

Her life is a series of unknown adventures. She cuts ties with all familial and material comfort and strides forth as a woman in men's clothes.

Sexy, beautiful, free. No ties.
    She is also lost, lonely and in exile. But this doesn't faze her.

*　*　*

- How much time do you spend on social media?
- Do you need to feel validated/witnessed/approved of in order to feel worthy?
- Do you celebrate your freedom?
- What are you tied to?
- What in life are you seduced by?

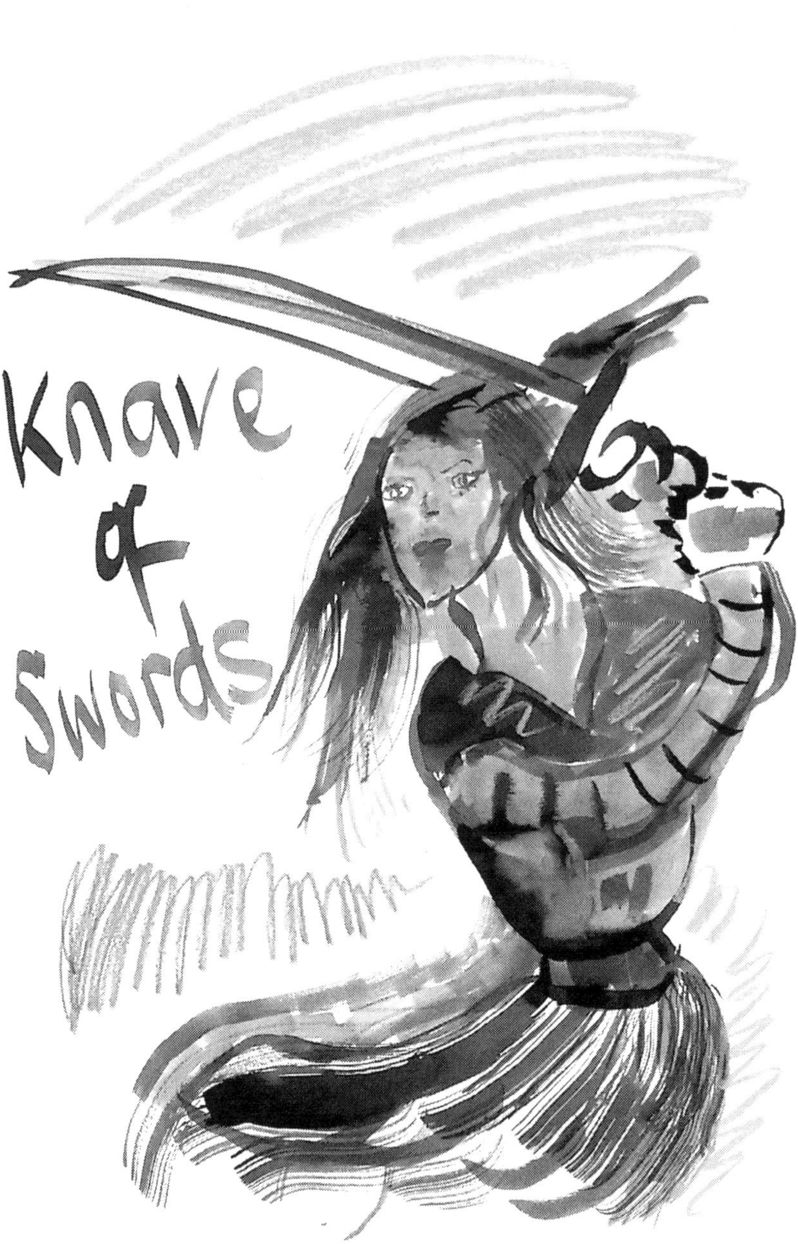
Knave of Swords

62

Knight of Swords

Incisiveness/Bluntness

There is an eagle in me that wants to soar, and there is a hippopotamus in me that wants to wallow in the mud.

-Carl Sandburg

This makes me think of the album title by Bill Callaghan *Sometimes I Wish We Were an Eagle*.

Swooping down onto our best ideas.

Noting down the poem that comes to us after a dream.
   Catching the wind quieting and settling after a storm.
   Meeting a stranger's eyes at the exact moment they look round at you.

Life coach to cupid and his arrow.

The Knight of Swords is a great accountability partner 'just effing do it'. The sweary version of the Nike slogan.
   Things don't get done unless we do them.

The Knight of Wands doesn't rate my trick of writing 'make a to do list' and the top of my to do list and ticking it off smugly.

No, he cannot abide procrastination of the nation.

He has very little patience, but what he lacks in this department he more than makes up for in 'getting shit done'.

I am calling on him to help me get this book birthed. I'm at that stage in the labour of the final push through the birthing canal. Writing is like pulling teeth or waiting for an eagle to fly me to the moon and back.

You see, he knows there is no creative breakthrough without a bit of a protesting push.

Sometimes I wish were were an eagle.

Flying above the drama we invent.

So often its not about us. We stand in the way of ourselves and forget that what we are doing is worthy of our time and that is why we are apprenticed to it.

Ideas come through us and we are lucky if one calls us. We must serve it.

***

- **Who do you wish you could be blunt with?**
- **What needs to catch your attention?**
- **What would make your heart soar?**
- **What needs a deadline?**

KNIGHT OF SWORDS

63

Queen of Swords

Perception/Sorrow

Every life has a measure of sorrow, and sometimes this is what awakens us.

-Steven Tyler

I'm sat on a bench in York town centre opposite a huge looming war memorial.

Its a bright Autumn morning and the copper and gold leaves that have fallen have blown and collected against the slate grey steps of the stern looking pyre.

Red poppy wreaths hang above with the logos of various Royal organisations.

Curling round above the sturdy old castle walls of York hover. On iron plaques there are many names spelled out in raised metal fonts.

Like the old type setting they used for printing.

At the beginning of the pandemic I wanted to say the names of the medical staff who died in service healing others from Covid.

I read this week about a beautiful 28- year old midwife from Texas who had just graduated, with her whole future ahead of her.

She was known in the wards for being relentlessly cheerful and singing through the corridors.

They did not have enough PPE so she re-used her mask so older, more at risk, staff could have new ones.

Within two months she'd had a full blood transfusion and was covered in tubes that she tried to rip out. Unconscious and on a ventilator, tears still poured from her swollen eyes when they played family phone message recordings.

When her parents were allowed in she was almost unrecognisable.

They switched her ventilator off.

The Queens of Swords is the Queen of Sorrows.

She is the war widow, the veteran nurse, the person whose job it is to assist families in switching off life support.

As I sit here on this rather bleak bench as people pass solemnly wearing their masks, the golden leaves tumbling sound like angels shuffling.

Death doulas.

It says carved into the stone THEIR NAME LIVETH FOR EVERMORE

* * *

- How can you perceive sorrow with joy?
- Whose names do you wish to honour?
- When did you last cry for lost love?
- How can you honour your past?
- Who are you still grieving?

QUEEN OF SWORDS

64

King of Swords

Wisdom/Intellectualism

An intellectual says a simple thing in a hard way. An artist says a hard thing in a simple way.

-Charles Bukowski

Interesting that upon pulling this card I immediately mislaid it. I think it's somewhere lodged down the back of our British Heart Foundation 80's, comfy, but oh so ugly teal sofa. Comfort is a great trade off for style.

If anyone was to judge my marriage by our upholstery the verdict would be comfortable, worn in, squishy and holding.

Make of that what you will.

Other relationships are plumper, cleaner, fluffier or even covered entirely in leather (oh yes) or matching scatter cushions (oh no). Not ours.

I think the King of Swords probably has a leather swivelly office chair. He's the guy who hires and fires and seems to do bugger all else yet still gets his own desk plaque and 'knock before entering' sign.

I guess we all need him. He hires who we need and pokes us with the tip of his sword in an effort to make us wake up to the people and situations who aren't serving us.

He's refreshingly ruthless and downright incisive.

I like to think of him as less Simon Cowell and more Zorro.

His fencing skills are second to none and he's slightly less neurotic and more reasonable than the old Queen of Hearts 'off with her head' type figures.

You see, his decision making is based on thoughtful reasoning not impulsiveness. He weighs things up.
    I have never considered myself an intellectual, but God knows I've tried to be one.

Dreams of being someone who gets paid to write their PhD or research some obscure statistic for 4 years.

But no. I am too distracted, whimsical and lazy to join the clever club.

Growing up, I had friends that got scholarships, went to Oxbridge universities or excelled without even trying.

I was a 'try your hardest' person. Never really shaking my early Essex roots or bad grammar habits but always overcompensating with quantity over quality.

I'd go the extra mile. Then completely wear myself out before the finish line.

I'd aim for a cool and stylish 'living space' then stick a disgusting green sofa in it. I tend to be great at hiring but not at firing.

This year my aim is for my pen to be sharper than my sword. Sword after all is word with an S at the front. The 'S' I think stands for silent.

Who says battles need to be spoken out loud? I can hire and fire with my written word. I don't need to be clever or have my own office.

***

- **When do you act like a Clever Clogs?**
- **When has your intellect served you?**
- **Do you recognize and acknowledge your creative intelligence and your emotional intelligence?**
- **Do you recognize the wise guide inside you?**
- **What is their advice for you?**
- **Write**
- **Read**
- **Write some more**

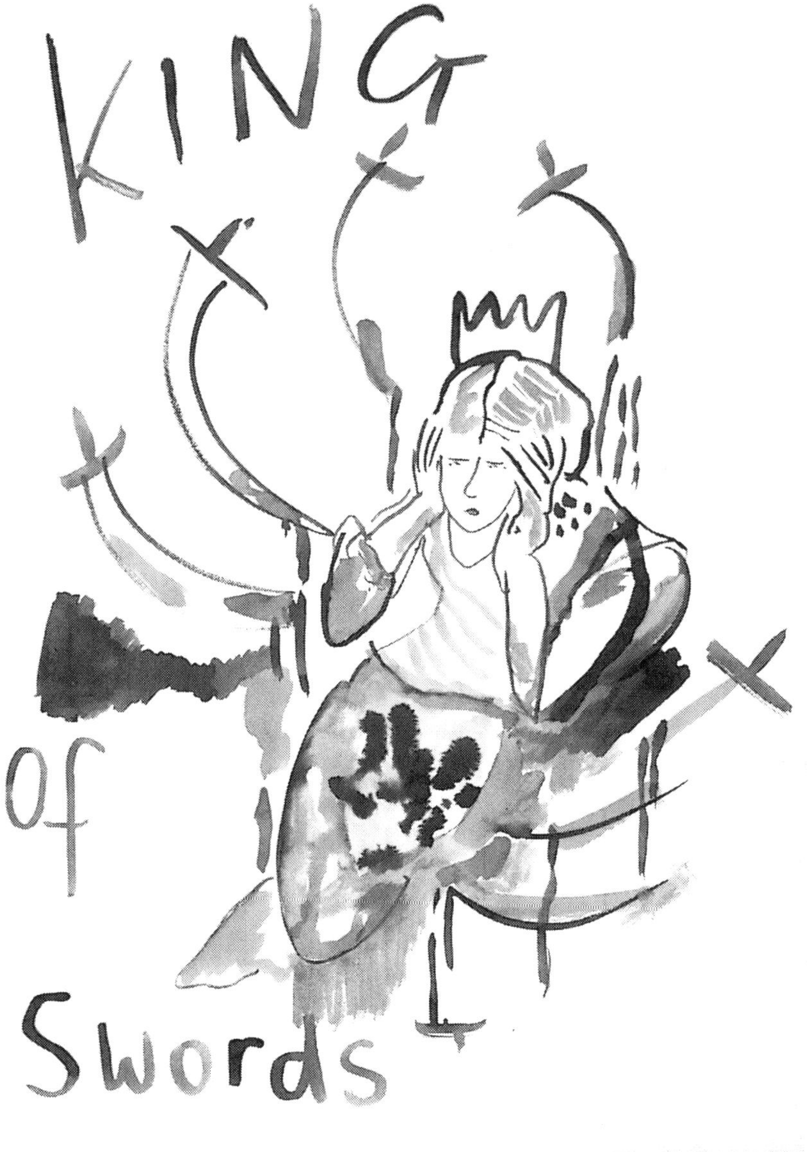
KING
of
Swords

65

Ace of Pentacles

Blessing/Obligation

Reflect upon your present blessings of which every man has many - not on your past misfortunes, of which all men have some.

-Charles Dickens

Reading John O' Donahue's book of blessings was beautiful this year. During the Covid crisis it was a great alternative to YouTube videos about the Keto diet or 24- day online courses about making origami penguins to fill the void.

Blessings.

Seems like an old fashioned word, doesn't it?

Like something you might whisper into an embroidered handkerchief or send by carrier pigeon with a loaf of daily bread.

'Bless' is something middle aged women say about cat videos. Or what people used to do when other people sneezed before we thought we might all get

Coronavirus.

Perhaps Boris should have changed his posters to '**catch it , kill it, bless it**'. Maybe then we wouldn't be in so much strife and peril.

When I first encountered Steiner education, I loved how the children would pray blessings over their food. Like everyday was harvest festival with blessed baked beans from the body of Christ (even if they were Asda's own brand).

Jesus loved a bargain.

* * *

- **What can you say 'thank you' for?**
- **What has blessed your day today?**
- **Who and what do you need to bless?**
- **Can you bless the difficulties you have encountered today?**
- **What has fed you today?**
- **What feels like an obligation?**

ACE OF PENTACLES

66

2 of Pentacles

Comparison/deliberation

Comparison is the thief of joy.

-Theodore Roosevelt

Katia didn't show up today. I felt her deliberation.
    The weather was wild and stormy. Storm Brendan I think.

Trees blew over.

I sat there feeling sad. I had so enjoyed our time together last week.

Red had met yellow in
    Orange on the thick snowy watercolour paper.

This week I had brought yellow and blue for us to meet in sea green strokes of emerald paint.
    She's slowly disappearing.
    Each week we meet in some rainbow on the canvas.

Meeting her in colours is a privilege.

I know she compares herself to everything and deliberates on every morsel I always bring her my best quality paints.

She deserves the finest things.

She thinks she deserves nothing

I sat there alone. Missing her. I moved my paintbrush through the blue and the yellow and in green I saw her eyes.

Nothing compares to you.

*　*　*

- **What could you afford yourself that you deserve?**
- **What colour do you want to float in, that you can simply receive?**
- **How are you comparing yourself with others?**

2 OF PENTACLES

67

3 of Pentacles

Performance/Variance

It's not how much money we make that ultimately makes us happy between 9 and 5. It's whether or not our work fulfils us.

- Malcolm Gladwell

This card is all about satisfaction in work.

Recently I led a group of 14 first-year therapy students into the myth of Medusa via mask work and a costumed performance.

This, I thought to myself, was the work I was born to do.

It's taken almost 38 years but I am finally earning (some) money from my purpose fuelled by passion.

It started eight years ago.

I'd lost my home and come out of an abusive relationship; destitute and mourning the loss of my dog best friend, Mavis the staffie, who was electrocuted after running onto a countryside railway track.

I'd lost almost everything including my dog.

I camped up in my mother's tiny damp spare room. Cried myself to sleep most nights.
   And wrote workshops.

I hired a local scout hut, continued working 12 hour bar shifts and got anyone, including my pub locals, to attend my weird theatrical workshops based on myth and fairy tale.

People always came back, had profound experiences, and my reputation grew as a weird and wonderful therapy lady who worked at the Red Lion, full of enchantment and great props.

Eventually I was approached by a drama therapist colleague to run a two year project with victims of domestic violence to use myth as a way to work with sexual and violent trauma.

The Red Shoes project was born. I got asked occasionally to give talks and lectures to therapy students and have recently had work published in journals.

Meanwhile I got work in a local primary school teaching art, and eventually met my now husband and moved into our rented 9th floor seafront flat.

I teach occasionally on the art therapy training course that I did.

I don't tend to share my story but my path of working in the therapy world has not been the usual academic route.

I trained for 3 years at the Tobias school or Art and Therapy and threw myself into finding my own god through art.

I have been in therapy for over 10 years and I am a certified wounded healer.

With Chiron and Medusa by my side I carve a way of being in this destructive world with my bow and arrow, stone setting eyes, snaky hair and ability to recognize a predator from a mile off.

I still have a long way to go, still paying off debts, teaching part time as I launch my freelance career, but I'm stable now. I've found a way to make my work a way to love others and offer something of deep personal value to the world.

* * *

- How can you honour yourself more deeply?
- What work calls to your soul?
- What jobs have you done that you enjoyed?
- How can you utilise your current work to enable your dreams?
- What do you feel is your true gift/value to the world
- Who needs your time and attention?
- What needs your time and attention?

3 of Pentacles

68

4 of Pentacles

Conservation/Greed

We are in danger of destroying ourselves by our greed and stupidity. We cannot remain looking inwards at ourselves on a small and increasingly polluted and overcrowded planet

- Stephen Hawking

The giant king sits awkwardly in the castle he has outgrown, I know this one.
　I tend to stay in jobs and relationships long after I've outgrown them.
　I wear tops from a decade ago.

I'd triple lock my castle door if I could.

I understand this card from a safety and comfort zone point of view but not a financial one. I never save for a rainy day, for example.
　This card's a bit like a fort.

A couple of years ago I really thought about the word *fort* and how *fortitude* sort of comes from it. It was a time when my boundaries, walls and forts were really crumbling.

I was feeling invaded, under siege.

I felt like I could not protect myself or my time.

Even friendships felt invasive. Not because my friends were awful. Simply because I needed some space,. I'd had a really full on time and needed to slam the brakes on, not hold endless banquets.

I was also struggling with debt. I'd just organized and paid for my own wedding.

I was running on empty, done in with chair covers, placeholders and welcome speeches.

Every part of my life needed fortification and a large do not disturb sign.

Since then I have done a few things:

- I try to fortify my family. Making sure I do visit/call/write to them and remember all birthdays. I also put them in my prayers and avoid them when I need to.
- I fortify my partnership. We try to maintain occasional dates and at least reserve one weekend morning for cuddles/ having a much needed argument or simply being lazy together in our home.
- I fortify my bank account. Simply by peeking at the dreaded bank balance regularly. Instead of chucking bank letters straight into the bin without opening them.
- I fortify my friendships. Sharing and caring and showing up or at least sending a text or a care package.
- I fortify my health. Meditation, nature and exercise. Occasional dentist visits.
- I fortify my work. Always working on inspiring self authored projects. Being as loving and creative in my job roles as I can. Remembering service is love. And life is service. *And work works best if you balance it*

with play.
- And most importantly I fortify me:

Spiritual support networks. Dance classes.
  Therapy.
  Days of doing fuck all. Chocolate.
  Forgiveness candles.
  Prayer.
  Nature. Wine.
  Lots of playtime. Theatre.
  City life. Art.
  Dance. Movies. Writing. Audio-books. Baths.
  Smoothies.

ALONE TIME.

Fortification doesn't mean building big fuck-off walls but it does mean laying solid foundations and putting the fuck-off walls up when you need to.

So that when one part of your life belly flops you are held tight by other things. You need your life to have your back.
  Don't just rely on mates.

They have their own fort battles going on.

* * *

<u>**Love is telling me....**</u>

That I'm tired of being the glue
The filler that smooths everything over
With my bubbly conversation

4 OF PENTACLES

And interpersonal skills
I'm too tired
I am being asked to step back and watch chaos unfold without intercepting
And making it ok for everyone
I am being asked to treasure and trust my own golden bowl of acorns
Not give them away
No more of my winter nourishment being stolen and spilt over the edges
By those who would leave me starved
I can still be generous but only to those who's golden thread doesn't wrap around mine and strangle it
I want to build a fort inside so that the outer walls
Don't need to be so stifling
I am bricks and mortar and love
But I am not glue
I will stand up for me
But I don't need to be anyone else's fort

* * *

- What needs your attention? Time? Love?
- What doesn't? Who do you need to protect yourself from right now? Be ruthless.
- Use your look-out towers.
- Peek through your battlements, have arrows ready to fire if need be. Keep your treasure safely guarded.
- Leave your castle from time to time. Invite nice people into it.
- Mess your castle up.
- Share your castle.
- Tidy it.
- Lock the doors.

- **Polish your floors.**
- **Keep your moat.**

That way you get to decide if it's worth your drawbridge coming down.

4 OF PENTACLES

69

5 of Pentacles

Poverty/Need

As long as poverty, injustice and gross inequality persist in our world, none of us can truly rest.

–Nelson Mandela

This card makes me think of food banks and the man who sleeps in the seafront bus shelter opposite my flat.

It's traumatised koalas being burnt in the Australian fires and people denied benefits who end up starving to death in uninhabitable council accommodation.

The people of China being forced into quarantine amidst disease fears. A sign of our times, the world we are sadly living in.
 I work with many people who need parenting more than their children do.
 Children who need constant entertainment and stimulation, normally via a screen. Anything but boredom.

5 OF PENTACLES

I pulled this card at 6.30 pm on a Tuesday.

I had worked 3 separate teaching jobs that day with over 50 pupils, done 10 pages worth of planning and assessment.

Run up 9 flights of steps to the small therapy room by the West Hill at the Wellbeing centre where I sometimes work.

Out of breath, I got the clay out. Lit a candle, poured a glass of water for my client. I didn't have time to pour my own.

Ran down the stairs to greet him so that he didn't have to do the stairs alone. 5 minutes past…19 minutes past…half an hour passed.
   My stomach rumbled, I hadn't eaten dinner, my head pounded. I went back up the 9 flights. No phone messages.
   Sometimes he just doesn't attend. No explanation.
   It's his only engagement with another person in the entire week. His only appointment with anything.
   He lives alone.

It was my 180th thing to do that day. I sat there feeling rejected and exhausted. He needed to stand me up. To make me less important I guess.
   By his absence I feel his presence. His denial of his own need.
   Some of us are time poor. Others company poor. Most of us forgiveness poor.

I will welcome him with open arms next week.

We all need each other and sometimes we are only recognised in our absence.

* * *

- **What are you scarce in? Time/money/love/rest/quiet?**
- **What do you really need that you are not getting?**
- **Do you feel resource rich or poor?**
- **Where is your energy getting depleted?**
- **Who makes you feel depleted?**

5 OF PENTACLES

70

6 of Pentacles

Liberality/ Manipulation

Unite liberality with a just frugality; always reserve something for the hand of charity; and never let your door be closed to the voice of suffering humanity.

-Patrick Henry

A large gold coin that looks like a medal. Surrounded by five others. Money and exchange are mentioned.

   I suppose this card is a gracious reminder that whatever I need is given. I often want more. But my needs are met well enough.

   I've learned to trust that just the right amount of people will attend my workshops. Enough to cover costs and materials and pay for a therapy session and a recovery chocolate bar to boot.

Just about earned enough this year to cover bills and debt repayments and fund the odd self development workshop.

Just enough super noodles in my cupboards, just enough love to see myself and others through hardship.

Just enough time to recover before returning to work each Monday. Just enough pebbles in the pot and wonders to re-fill the well.

The wonderful balance of just enough. No more. No less.

Just the right things found in charity shops and gifted to me in perfect time and space. Life is so generous.
   Seal shaped stones found on beaches and pressed flowers found in my mother's old books.

Our culture often incites greed. We want bigger kitchens, sexier lingerie, skinnier hips, bulging wallets, heavier holiday allowance and more voluminous hair.

We want cheap flights, ashram yoga experiences, season tickets, 2-for-1 pizza deals, coffee coupons, spa days, musicals, maxi lashes, mini manicures.

Endless gain.

What we need is less spending, more silence and space to simply breathe gratitude into what we have.

Rather than seeking and finding more.

Less, after all - say many shrewd designers - is more.

And we are just enough.

* * *

* * *

- **What do you have enough of?**
- **How can you be more generous?**
- **How can you trust that life gives you exactly what you need?**
- **What can you give away?**

6 OF PENTACLES

71

7 of Pentacles

Re- evaluation/Melancholy

What's the first thing I do when I wake up in the morning? Wish I hadn't.

-Morrissey

It started when I dredged myself out of bed to do my 'morning exercise routine'.

My bras don't fit…as I can't face the horror of having my sagging tits measured by an M&S employee in a nylon skirt with a name badge that reads 'Debra- 35 years service', or worse, 17- year old Aleisha with no boobs and only 6 months service between her A Level exams.

So in my ill-fitting crop top, I attempt slack high kicks to 'Rhythm is a Dancer'. Everything just jiggles and hurts.

'*You can feel it everywhere*'.

Some people say exercise helps you feel great. Wine and ice cream work better for me.

Just star jumps without proper cup support.

But, its not Cups, its Pentacles....7 of Pentacles.

Sending out emails in my terrible neon, nylon exercise clothes, I messaged someone about a great sad film I had watched with a box of Kleenex, then burst into tears at the memory of it.

So much melancholy. I attract it.

My supervisor notices I tend to attract more sad clients than angry ones.

Shortly after said supervisor meeting, I jump in a cab to go home and, following my polite 'its a bit cloudy today' conversation starter, the driver stops car and bursts into tears talking about his depressed mother. I literally just leech out peoples sadness just by talking about weather.

I am a magnet for sad sacks. 'Mad for Sadness' (a great B-side from melancholy Glaswegian band Arab Strap).

The melancholy in me knows the melancholy in you.

My husband is an ex emo kid. He spent years making his dyed black hair cover one smudged eye-linered eye with just the right slick of misery.

I meanwhile spent my youth listening to the droning tones of The Smiths and smoked roll-ups with a rolled up skirt, in bus stops that smelled of piss. A perfect way to waste a day.

Cure lyrics etched into tree barks with keys. Record fairs full of shoe gazers in a world without Spotify. Mosh pits full of grease and sweat. Nervous phone box calls and knock off band tshirts outside the Camden Palace.

This card, the 7 of Pentacles, suggests missed opportunities. Phone numbers not procured. Moments not seized, lost hopes.

The rose is at his melancholic feet and he doesn't know.

Too busy looking in the distance to find someone on Plenty of Fish to give it to.

Pining after ex girlfriends and the perpetually unavailable Victoria's Secret models (with perfectly supported cups) that evade his pentacle tentacles.

Melancholy was with me today. In the prising wind. The cold sea. The whistling buildings.

A teen in my art therapy confidence building group drew a wet dog dripping under an umbrella in leaky biro. Confidence is only an umbrella anyway.

Today is the first day of my new writing challenge. I always try to beat the blues in January by signing up for some new thing to fail at.

This year it's writing. It's day one and melancholy and doubts are high. Self esteem is low. If only I could recognise the red rose at my feet.

***

- **What makes you melancholy?**
- **What do you like about Autumn?**
- **When was the last time you indulged in your sadness?**
- **Make a great sad playlist**
- **Wear muted colours**
- **Write a love song for your exes**

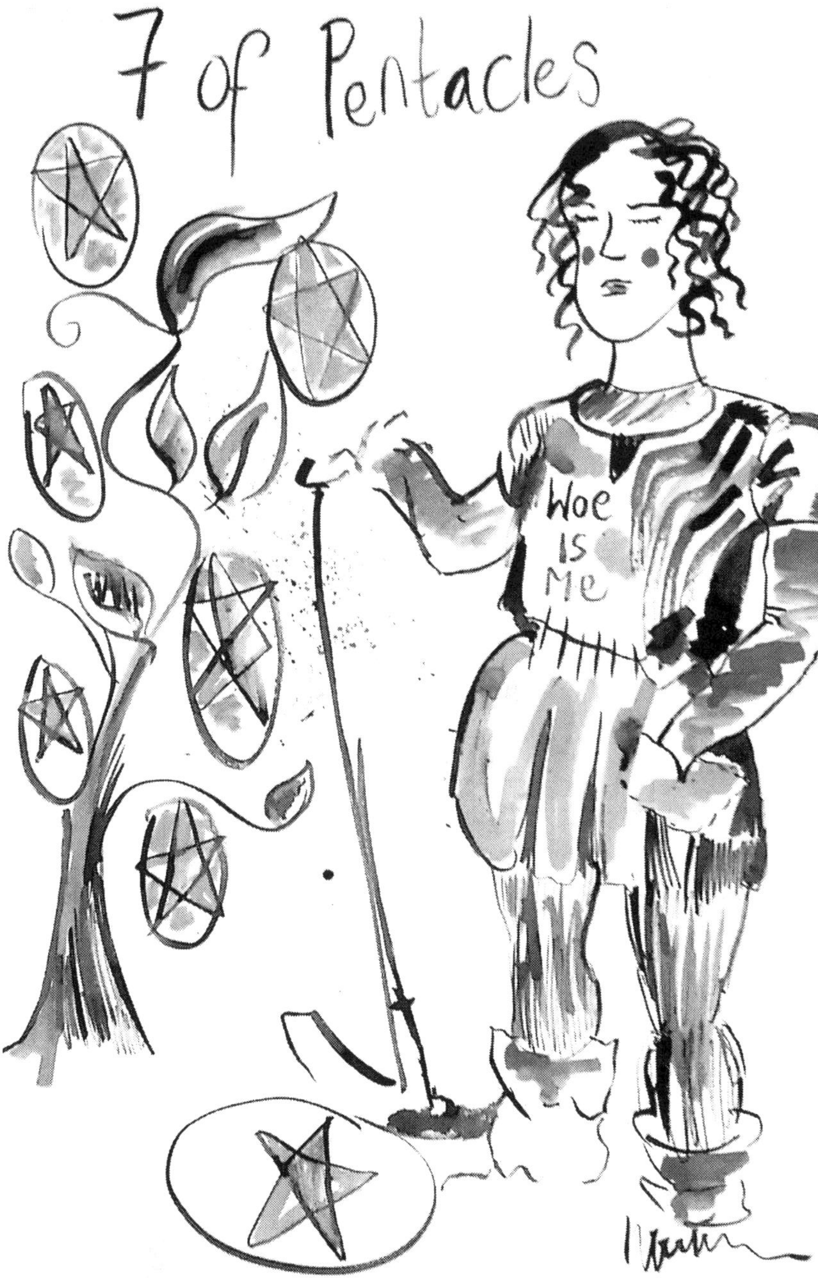
7 of Pentacles
Woe
is
Me

72

8 of Pentacles

Craftsmanship/Compliance

Sometimes history takes things into its own hands.

-Thurgood Marshall

This card reminds me of my great uncle John.

He was a carpenter and joiner. Bit of an electrician.

Dabbled with watercolours and could play any theme tune of my favourite TV shows on my Casio keyboard despite having zero music training. He played by ear alone.

Left school at 14.

Fought in the Second World War.

He drank strong tea and smoked Golden Virginia roll ups.

He had a heart made of gold, lungs made of tar, dirty vests and a huge propensity for worry. His daughter still used to have to phone him to tell him she got home safe at 50.

He loved my sister and me and we *adored* him.

My aunt told me once that she was prevented from being close to him as a

child as her mother was possessive of his love.
This made me very sad.

Years after he died I looked at some old family photos. I kept seeing this strange woman in all of them.
When I asked mum about her, mum confided that she was a family friend that my Uncle had an affair with for years.
It wasn't ever talked about afterwards. She stopped appearing in the photos.

In my head that marriage had been perfect. They had been married for 50 years, from the age of 16.
This family secret shocked me.
The way both parties bore it without ever giving a hint of it away in their daily interactions.
They treated my sister and me like the beloved innocent children we were. Never putting their stuff on us.
I see so many parents confiding in their poor kids.
It's so important to protect children from adulthood sometimes.

Great uncle John worked so bloody hard.
Hammer and nail. Minimum wage. Odd-job man. Worked for free for friends.
Of course he had to break free.
Like Freddie Mercury in pink lipstick. The mystery woman is a family ghost.

It's OK. All families have them.
I know none of us were any less loved.

* * *

- What can you make with your own hands?
- What is your craft?
- Can you make a cake? Do DIY? Play a tune? Fix something broken?
- Where have you complied?
- How can you break free?
- What family patterns/conventions do you wish to break?

8 OF PENTACLES

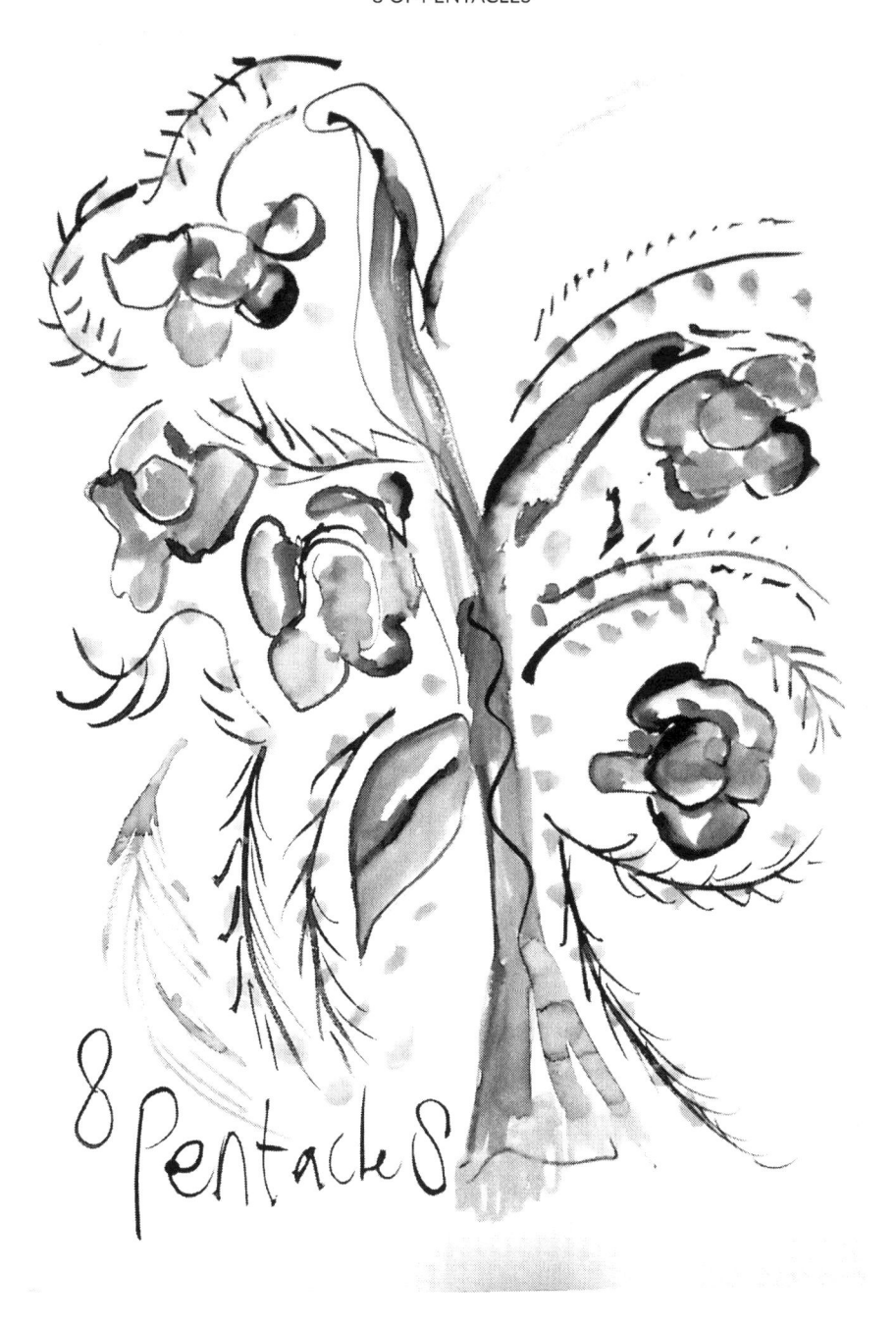

73

9 of Pentacles

Discipline/Overconfidence

Dictators fall when they're overconfident; they stay in power when they're paranoid.

-Masha Gessen

This week I entered into a week long training with the amazing Jonathan Kay to explore the archetype of the fool. Essentially, this is a process of undermining overconfidence and finding the discipline to disciple my wild twin. The one without intelligence, over confidence or smart arse, clever clogs tricks.
 The part that's flawed and vulnerable.

Why on earth would I want to spend half term at a fooling workshop on Zoom?

I asked myself this question roughly once every ten seconds throughout the five day training.

I squirmed throughout. Every fibre of my resistance was activated.

Jonathan, who's dedicated his life to this work, talks in strange word riddles like the Professor in Narnia who knows the children can slip between worlds.

This week something incredible happened.

In the last hour of the five long days I saw a glimpse of it:

The fool with the nine gold coins or tears.

Jonathan explained that I had shot my fool many many times.

'After all he is everything you are not.'

The wild twin. The one that stands beneath us. Who understands. Under stand... to stand under.
   Was this a week of understanding the shapes of my humiliation? Yes.

But humiliation is connected to humility.

To be more human.

And human, he said, 'means bearer of light'.

I think I caught a glimpse of this light. That I carry all the time but constantly cover and recover with my thinking (JK calls it the thin king).

Jonathan reminded me that my fool lives in the everydayness of things.

He's outside the hierarchy of the King and Queen who run the show.

'Extraordinary just means extra ordinary'.

He reminded us to stick with the mundane (and often profane) in order to find the sacred scared and scarred worlds beneath.

All of my shame and hurt and covered over bits.

'Be the crumpled version of yourself' he said to a very well put together participant.

So five days were spent crumpling.
   I cracked and swore, secretly under my Zoom camera and tears poured forth.

'Oh you're just defrosting' he said with the kindest eyes.

Then I did a 20 minute uninterrupted improvised piece where I surprised myself most of all.

Where the hell did that come from?

My fool. He goes where angels fear to tread.

This workshop was not soft or fluffy or easy or even fun.

It was real. And I used my real eyes. Realise.

I think my fool is the one I've been longing for.
   To be longing is to belong.

This is not about therapy but it is a way to stay humble and see the words we choose to use as spells. In a profession where we think we might play the part of wise counsel:

'The fool doth think he is wise, but the wise man knows himself to be a fool.'

9 OF PENTACLES

Sometimes we have to undermine ourselves to find the gold. Nine gold coins. To be a disciple to ourselves and shoot down the kings and queens who rule our kingdoms.

Maybe there the small red bird will sing.

*　*　*

- **How are you overly confident?**
- **How does this undermine the shy, unexplored parts of you?**
- **How can you discipline yourself to be a real beginner at something?**
- **What nine gold coins would be the new things you would like to try if you weren't embarrassed?**

THE WONKY WOMAN'S GUIDE TO TAROT

IX Nine of Pentacles

74

10 of Pentacles

Abundance/Extravagance

Doing what you love is the cornerstone of having abundance in your life.

-Wayne Dyer

How can we feel this if we have a strong poverty consciousness? Sounds a bit new-age hippy-dippy right? Well you're reading a tarot book so I'll assume you've heard these terms before by money manifesting gurus.

My dad grew up with an outside toilet. My husband was bathed in washing-up liquid. My mum used loans to pay off other loans and sewed her own clothes including her school uniform.

This is in my bones.

I skimp on food shopping. I buy everything in the sales or charity shops.

My sister famously jokes that in my student days I reused tea bags.

So what's it like for me when financial abundance comes my way?

I spend it immediately. A course, a weekend away, an extravagant birthday gift, a book buying splurge.

You see in my head, money's not for having or hoarding but spending.

It slips through my fingers.

I wish I was less of a hoarder in other aspects. The teacher I've been working with this week says we collect trophies.

Trophies all around us.

Totems of experience; yet in and of themselves they are empty.

Empty vessels offering themselves to us to fill with memory.

What's the difference between an idea and an offer he asked me.

Well, I replied, 'an offer is something we receive in grace.'

'An idea is something we construct.'

To offer is to present or proffer something) for (someone) to accept or reject as desired.

To have an idea is a thought that leads to a possible course of action.

I guess the main difference being is that the offer comes from the outside, from someone or something else.

And the idea comes from inside our heads.

So when an offer and an idea collide there is something of the inner and outer worlds meeting.

Making our stories come to life.

Perhaps to live extravagantly with a sense of abundance is to recognise the offers that life constantly make us.

To fuse these with ideas and grace and possibility.

To give up the trophies and simply be 'in it to win it'.

Because if we are truly in our own life we are winning at it.

With the wind in our sails and the earth at our feet.

I think we earn our abundance crowns from those we love and those who love us.

I am not a money magnet but a miracle magnet.

Charged with love.

***

- **How could you be more extravagant?**
- **What miracles have you attracted today?**
- **What feels scarce?**
- **Make a gratitude list.**
- **Make a wish list.**

THE WONKY WOMAN'S GUIDE TO TAROT

75

Knight of Pentacles

Practicality/Waste

I think the chance of finding beauty is higher if you don't work on it directly. Beauty in architecture is driven by practicality. This is what you learn from studying the old townscapes of the Swiss farmers.

-Peter Zumthor

I went to British Heart Foundation shop today.
    Bought three autumn dresses and pair of tan cowgirl boots.

'Waste not want not'.

Most of my clothes come from charity shops.

Zara, Hobbs, Jigsaw, were today's designer finds.

I went to Tunbridge Wells today, hence the fancy labels.

Twin-sets and neat hems.

They are all a pain in the arse to wash, requiring dry cleaning and low temperatures.

But who cares when they are £5?

My Mum had a minor heart op last week.

My autumn wardrobe will make me think of her and has probably paid for some atrium tubing.

Leaves fall and my rusty coloured skirt hems sit just above my cross legged knee, where a chill sits.

When winter comes I'll still wear brown and mustard.

Autumn colours suit my genes, hereditary like the heart flutters, leaves falling.

* * *

- What can you 'waste not want not'?
- What could you recycle into something fabulous?
- What in your life is both comfortable and practical?
- List five very simple luxuries each day

KNIGHT OF PENTACLES

76

Knave of Pentacles

Caution/Carelessness

Throw caution to the wind and just do it.

-Carrie Underwood

'Throw caution to the wind' my friend said. She beckoned me into the water naked and pale under the moonlight.

'Slip under, it's warm!', she squealed.

I crossed my arms tight over my chest.

I rarely do nakedness.
    Haven't stripped off in front of anyone for too long.

I feel vulnerable and exposed but I slip my pants off and slide into the beckoning soft waves.

It is surprisingly warm for late August and I feel the moonlight highlighting me.

I feel radiant as the water washes over me waist deep, over my hips, a little deeper covering my pale breasts.

I feel like a real woman. A real sealion selkie.

Shimmering skin. Luminous and wet.

The salt water cleanses and heals my sores.

I feel alive again.
   Caution has been thrown to the wind. I'm not a great swimmer but I stand still and feel the movement of the water meeting and caressing me.

I see a bunch of teens up on the promenade. Suddenly I don't care anymore. I feel free.

Careless and beautiful, my swollen sea body with a silver moon between my salty thighs.

* * *

- **What can you say 'fuck it!' to?**
- **Get naked**
- **Swim in the sea**

THE WONKY WOMAN'S GUIDE TO TAROT

knave of pentacles

77

Queen of Pentacles

Comfort/ Laziness

If you look for truth, you may find comfort in the end; if you look for comfort you will not get either comfort or truth only soft soap and wishful thinking to begin, and in the end, despair.

C. S. Lewis

Day three of no bra. Day eight of unwashed hair.
   Ten unwashed coffee cups.
   A pile of unread books by the bed.
   Abandoned hair ties.
   Jogging bottoms everyday.

Unwritten letters.
   Unwritten to do lists.

Let alone crossing anything off.

The only thing I am crossing off are the days which could well turn into months and unspent years.

On Facebook people are posting their dewy faced 20 year old selves.

I unearth a picture of me in Peckham Rye park with a jaunty feather accentuating my curly thick hair.
   Slim shoulders. Alabaster skin.

She knew not her beauty.
   At the time I'd just had an abortion.
   Having been shagging some guy on my uni course who wouldn't even call me his girlfriend.

We'd drink beer, draw comics together in chunky marker pens that smelt of solvents and have sex in the middle of the day.

Hedonistic times.

I was lost in being lost.

So in love with love.

From this place of isolation my nostalgia is palpable.

I am grieving the babies I haven't had.
   Especially that one.

That implanted itself in my womb only to be washed away.

Like the alcohol washed down.

Girls under waterfalls.

Comics about inertia.

Now I'm in my own inertia comic.

Making Facebook lives in my dressing gown. Drinking wine at 4pm on a Sunday.

Letting my greying hair fall over my more burdened swollen shoulders as I dance like I wish everybody was watching.

Drinking down chia seed smoothies in my kitchen like they were shots on a dark dancefloor.

I think of Peckham Rye and remember that William Blake had visions there.

I write sonnets to that girl full of pregnant light.

From my dressing gown.

* * *

- **What takes you out of your comfort zone?**
- **Can you give yourself a lazy day without guilt?**
- **What do you take comfort in?**
- **How are you cutting corners in your life?**

Queen of Pentacles

78

King of Pentacles

Possession/Acquisition

We are all born into the world with nothing. Everything we acquire after that is profit.

-Sam Ewing

I have an instant dislike of this card. Makes me think of property developers and people who love playing Monopoly, buying hotels on the purple squares.

I've rebelled against this archetype. I have no assets and am prepared to rent my whole life.

I had an abusive relative who used money to be cruel. He would use money as a weapon. He thought that because he earnt money he could be a legitimate arsehole and that buying awful properties and making us move house was love.

It wasn't. It just meant we had to start again and sell our beloved pets.

My mum has huge debt problems. My sister too. I dealt with it all by refusing to want any financial security.

I've lived in illegally parked caravans that got set fire to, lived off baked beans even in my 30's, never had a car. Lived in broken properties infested with vermin, damp, leaky buildings; currently my front door doesn't function.

I don't do financial security or acquisition. Neither does my husband.
   BUT...

We always go to the theatre. Usually weird fringe stuff. It's actually cheaper than a takeaway most times.

We eat out on special occasions.

We travel by coach and train round Europe every summer. We camp.
   I go to countless soul feeding workshops or if I can't afford to go to them, I run countless soul feeding workshops.

I buy everything from charity shops.

I have shares in yellow sticker aisles. Poundland is my Disneyland.
   And we live way beyond our means.

Life is rich. There are always days full of free museums and nature walks to look forward to and our rented rickety flat looks out onto the ocean.
   Perhaps the King of Pentacles is in my life. He wears rags made of rainbows.

* * *

- **What rags have you made into rainbows?**
- **How are you thrifty?**
- **What are your financial assets?**

- **What are your creative assets?**
- **Make a gratitude list of 100 things you are grateful for**

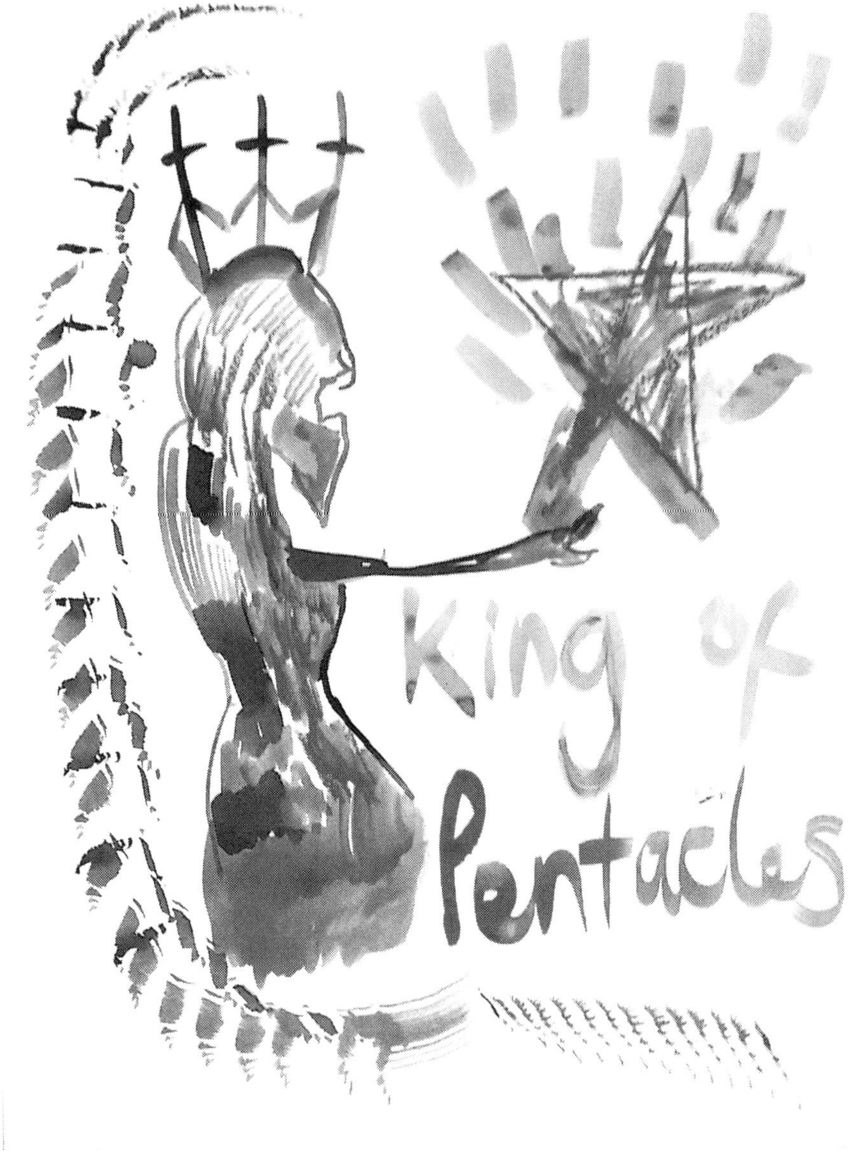
King of
Pentacles

Afterword

And these are suns— vast central living fires—
Lords of dependent systems— kings of worlds
That wait as satellites upon their power,
And flourish in their smile. Awake, my soul,
And meditate the wonder! Countless suns
Blaze round thee, leading forth their countless worlds!
Worlds in whose bosoms living things rejoice.
And drink the bliss of being from the fount
Of all-pervading Love!

-From *An introduction to the Study of the Heavens* by Hannah M. Bouvier, 1858

* * *

Acknowledgements

Thank you to Leonie Dawson, Debbie Reeds, Dave Rock, the three Jonathan's: Clements, Brown, and Kay, all teachers who gave me the kind kick up the arse I needed this year.

To everyone at Eggtooth's Resonate, especially Laura Dunton Clark - None of this would have happened without this awesome platform.

Thank you to all my clients past, present and future, my deepest most beautiful teachers.

Leonie Guest and Nick Williams my most trusted anchors.

Thank you to my eternally loving partner Triston Spicer for helping me in a zillion sweet ways and putting up with my creative messes all over our tiny flat and proofreading and scanning like a boss.

Thank you to supportive girlfriends particularly Melanie Lowndes, Juliet Kenny, Sarah Bullock, Liane Shenfield, Steph Norris, Bella Todd, Hazel Etteridge, Thilaka Hillman, Pheone Cave, The Friern Road crew, Kerry Hopkinson, Hollie and Lizzie, Consolations book club, everyone in Presence of Love Monday group and all the folks on my Speckled Eggs and Feathers page.

To Alice Grist (read all her Tarot books-she's wonderful) for inspiring me with her Cosmic Mother deck painted with her children.

For all the children and young people I work with who bring endless joy to my life without me being an actual mother.

For ART and WRITING my twin saviours for ever.

For the Artists Way and A Course in Miracles my guiding spiritual texts that keep me on the straight and narrow and in creative recovery.

Also, last but not least my family especially my mum, Wendy Atkinson. Your love is what I owe all my creativity to.

Many names and details in this book have been fictionalized to maintain confidentiality.

ACKNOWLEDGEMENTS

* * *

Teacher Acknowledgment

For Liz
   I met you after midsummer this August
   When the sea was still swimable
   When the evening light lingered
   Long
   You spoke and your words were so heavy
   So real
   Every part of you was worthy
   You told us you had just 6 weeks left
   Your liver was ruined
   That was the length of my school holiday this year
   But you carried on regardless
   You spoke with such surety
   You spoke of reverance
   Gladness even
   Inspiration
   Through wisdom
   You were so brave
   So together
   Even though you knew it was all falling apart inside
   You spoke and I recieved you
   So so privileged I was
   To hear you
   To meet you
   You taught me what a teacher should be
   The gratitude for this service

TEACHER ACKNOWLEDGMENT

I learnt today that your body finally left the classroom of this life
I know every student of yours will be bereft
I will be
And I met you once
Thankyou for being

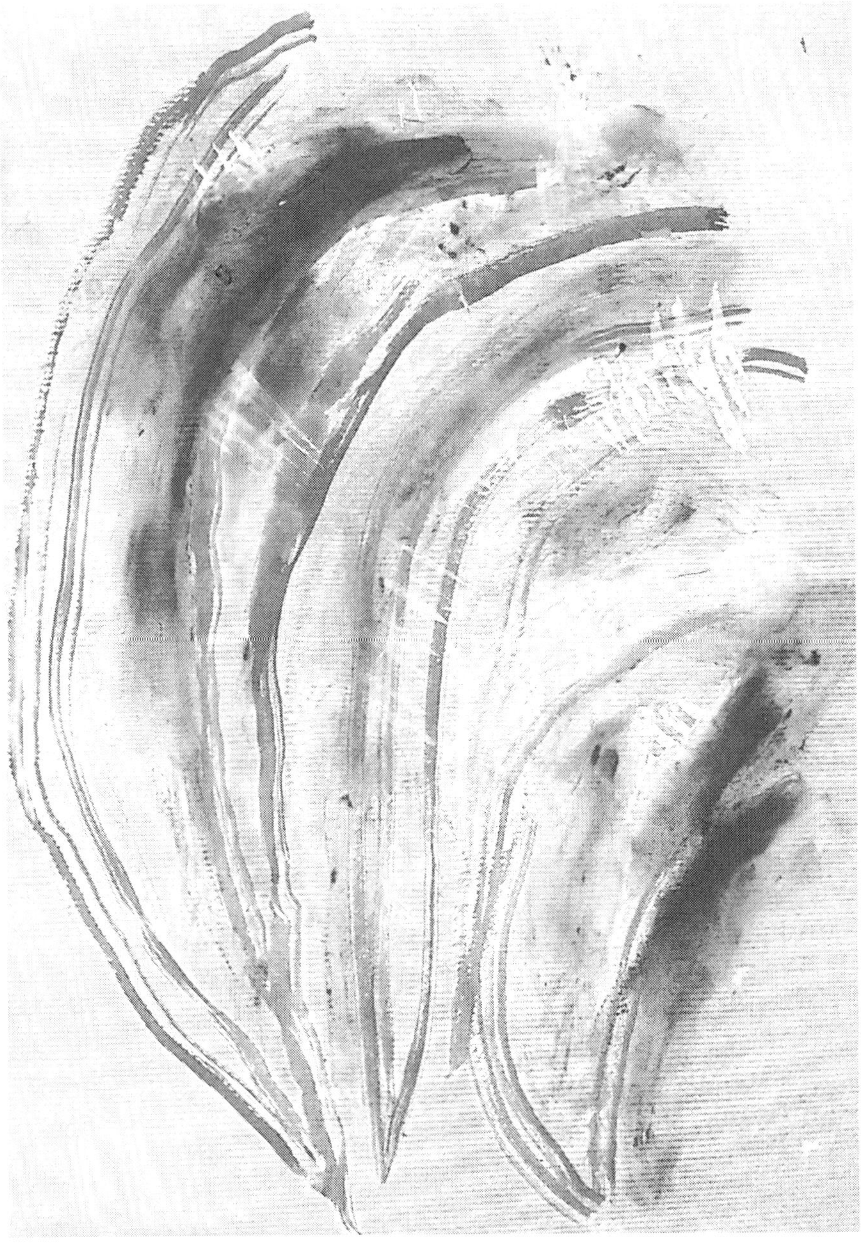